SCIENCE AND RELIGION

As the world approaches the twenty-first century beset with mounting global problems, the remnants of the age-old conflict between science and religion have taken on the form of shackles, producing a stalemate and a paralysis of will. In debunking a number of scientific and religious dogmas, the author attempts to clear the ground for the laying of new foundations of a society in which science and religion can resume their old harmony.

Anjam Khursheed is a research physicist at CERN, the European Organisation for Nuclear Research in Geneva. He graduated in 1979 with honours in physics from Edinburgh University, where he went on to receive his PhD. He has written a number of scientific papers on particle physics and electromagnetic fields.

SCIENCE
AND
RELIGION

*Towards the Restoration
of an
Ancient Harmony*

Anjam Khursheed

ǁONEWORLDǁ
PuBLiCATioNS

SCIENCE AND RELIGION
Towards the Restoration of an Ancient Harmony

Oneworld Publications Ltd
1c Standbrook House, Old Bond Street, London W1X 3TD
PO Box 1908, Limassol, Cyprus

© Anjam Khursheed 1987

Reprinted 1987

British Library Cataloguing in Publication Data
Khursheed, Anjam
Science and Religion: towards the restoration of an ancient harmony
1. Religion and science
I. Title
215   BL240.2

ISBN 1-85168-005-5

Printed in Great Britain by
The Guernsey Press Co. Ltd, Guernsey, Channel Islands

'When we consider what religion is for mankind, and what science is, it is no exaggeration to say that the future course of history depends upon the decision of this generation as to the relations between them. We have here the two strongest general forces — apart from the mere impulse of the various senses — which influence men and they seem to be set one against the other, the force of our religious intuitions, and the force of our impulse to accurate observation and logical deduction.'

Alfred North Whitehead

CONTENTS

INTRODUCTION: *Profane Religion, Sacred Science*   1

1. DISCOVERING THE MATERIAL WORLD   5

The Greek Heritage   6
The Impact of Christianity and Islam   15
From the Renaissance to the Modern World   27
Scientific Method and Religious Insight   39

2. HUMAN EVOLUTION: *By Accident or Design?*   55

Materialistic Theories of Evolution   56
Criticisms of the Materialist View   65
The Model of Evolution Applied to Society   80
A New Model of Evolution and Design   87

3. THE MEETING OF TWO WAYS   99

New Horizons of the Material Realm   99
A New Physics and a New Religion   112
Complementarity in Science and Religion   117

Notes   121

Bibliography   125

Index   129

Introduction
Profane Religion, Sacred Science

The past four hundred years have taught us to think of science and religion as pitifully unequal contestants in a struggle for our hearts and minds. It has been above all a contest over which will show us the true nature of our world and our existence in it. The scientists seem to have won. With a stunning succession of theories they have appeared to oust one by one the religious teachings on these questions. Today, many people in the West firmly believe that religion is at best an outmoded set of values and beliefs — once useful to more primitive society but no longer necessary — and at worst it represents a set of superstitious dogmas which cause considerable conflict and strife in the world.

Science also seems to have won a kind of moral contest. It has had the humility to lay all of its pronouncements open to the freest criticism, demanding nothing to be taken on faith or as a matter of obligation. Religion, by contrast, has often prided itself on the infallibility of its doctrines, making its beliefs exempt from revision and, at certain points in history, not hesitating to impose them by torture and burning at the stake. Because science has a method for choosing rationally between rival theories, it has progressed peacefully and brought together people of every nation, race and tradition in a harmonious quest for knowledge. Religion, however, has often clung to outmoded visions and has divided people against each other in a deafening quarrel between conflicting dogmas. It also stands accused of making false promises by speaking of eternal rewards for the faithful. According to some thinkers, these promises are best understood as instruments of social oppression by which ruling social élites retain the obedience of exploited classes and secure their resignation to inadequate earthly rewards.

In its original Latin sense, 'profane' means 'outside the temple'. It is as though we have made of our civilisation a temple to science, with scientists as the priests of the New Age, and it is now religion that stands outside. To speak well of religion has even become a way of using language tastelessly; the old distinction between the sacred and the profane has been inverted. From our great distance in time, it is easy to lose sight of the fact that even this distinction did not always hold. When European religion was transformed in the Christian era into a hierarchical, authoritarian structure, it became obligatory for inquiry to fix its gaze almost exclusively on the divine. For almost a millenium before, however, Greek thinkers had freely pursued religious insight, philosophical abstraction and scientific investigation in a single quest for nourishment of the soul. Religion was to be found outside the temple as much as science, and both were sacred.

It is true that science progressed slowly in the days of this ancient harmony. It is also true that in order to become the great gift that it is today it has had to go through a period of conflict with the religious and philosophical preconceptions that held it back. No one would want to return, out of an unscientific nostalgia, to the days before Galileo and Newton. The purpose of this present work, however, is to help loosen − if only to a modest degree − the hold on so many minds of the familiar picture painted in the opening paragraph above of victor and vanquished in a spiritual war between science and religion. It argues for the desirability of a resurrection of that ancient harmony which was a forward-looking and progressive one, and points to the first scientific hints of its re-emergence.

Chapter 1 relates a story of science quite properly in conflict with the religion of a particular time and place. Against a background of philosophical and religious obstacles, a revolution in thinking in the seventeenth century established a scientific method of investigating the material world. This was an immense step forward, and it could not be taken without dislodging the Church from its claim to have the last word in all questions of human understanding. The resulting conflict, which in various forms persists today, was caused not by any essential incompatibility between science and religion, but rather by the first confrontation between modern science and the corrupted and dogmatic religion of the Dark Ages. In contrast, the flourishing of sciences and arts in the Islamic Civilisation of the same era is cited as historical evidence against the theory that religion possesses an intrinsic quality that requires it to be in conflict with science and progress. That the conflict continues is more correctly attributed to fundamental misconceptions regarding the true purpose and nature of both science and religion, misconceptions which have distorted our perception of the harmony which has always existed between them.

Chapter 2 presents a picture of scientific theory overreaching itself, attempting unnecessarily and without justification to oust religious belief on the questions of human origins and human destiny. Our focus moves to the nineteenth and twentieth centuries and their mechanistic theory of evolution. It is undeniable that life has evolved, but the evolutionary mechanism that the nineteenth century has handed down to us as scientifically given – that evolution is blind and its *sole* cause is the survival of chance mutations – cannot be proven by scientific method. Any such mechanism would leave the evolutionary process without meaning, and humankind without purpose. Extensions of the survivalist evolutionary model to other areas of inquiry, such as social theory, have tended to reinforce this despairing conclusion.

Chapter 3 looks at some of the most recent developments in scientific theories as they relate to traditional concepts of the origin and nature of the universe. In the twentieth century research in physics has brought about repeated and profound changes in our conception of science and of the universe. The doctrine of mechanistic determinism has been found to be an unhelpful guide to our understanding as we delve deeper into the secrets of the material world, and within the new theories of physical nature can be heard other intriguing echoes of religious insights which have gone before them. These developments offer the possibility of a new under-standing of the relationship between science and religion, one that resolves and transcends their past conflicts.

This work is inspired partly by the Bahá'í Faith, and partly by some thought-provoking modern developments in scientific research. The Bahá'í Faith is an all too little known world religion, founded in Iran in the 1840's. Not only is it a surprisingly open-minded and progressive religion to have appeared in that particular time and place, but its principles stand in our own day as a challenge to the assumptions of twentieth-century society. Among them is the teaching that we should follow both our scientific and our religious impulses. In the words of 'Abdu'l-Bahá, son of the religion's founder, science and religion are like two wings on which the human race will take flight like a bird. With only one wing — religion — to lift us towards enlightenment, we must fall back into a slough of superstition. With only the other — science — to hold us aloft, we must succumb to a despairing materialism.[1] The three chapters of this book offer three glimpses of the history of science, and discuss them in the light of this teaching. However, no attempt is made to introduce the Bahá'í Faith in its broader aspects. A number of books of that nature already exist.[2]

The author does not claim to be an expert on all aspects of the subject discussed in the following pages, nor does he claim to have written a definitive work on the relationship between science and religion or on the complex question of human evolution. However, it is hoped that what is written here may engender interest and stimulate discussion, and thereby contribute to our understanding.

1. DISCOVERING THE
MATERIAL WORLD

'As one goldfish said to another: "Of course there is a God! Who do you think changes the water?"'

At the end of the sixteenth century a new way of thinking brought about a revolution in scientific method and achievement. It was as though human beings were discovering for the first time the material world that had been philosophically downgraded for so long. For the previous two thousand years material things had been deemed of little interest to investigators. Seekers after knowledge who wanted to uncover conceptually rigorous and mathematically precise features of reality had thought that only objects of pure thought were capable of such regularity. This turning of inquiry away from material physical nature suited the religious vision of the Middle Ages, and the Church readily froze an evolving Greek picture of the world – one which in former times had always looked forward to bettering itself through free discussion and open criticism – into a rigid doctrine. Science made its breakthrough by overturning the ancient view of the material world and by persisting in questioning established views about nature, even when the Church invested its authority in maintaining them.

It seems almost impossible to look back to those times without a feeling of impatience at the backward thinking that had to be overcome. This is to forget, however, that Greek and medieval abstract thinkers developed highly valuable conceptual tools, especially in mathematics. Without them the scientific revolution would have been a sheer impossibility; and since these very inventors of science and mathematics were chiefly motivated by a Greek religious impulse, not to mention the later work carried out by Islamic mathematicians, astronomers and physicians, religion cannot be considered wholly pernicious. We may also ask ourselves: if the Greeks, with all their subtlety of mind, were capable of so badly underrating the investigation of things material, are we not also capable, despite our own great understanding, of seriously overrating this investigation, to the disadvantage of other forms of wisdom?

The Greek Heritage

No single strong aristocracy or priest class existed in ancient Greece to impose one Greek way of thinking, and yet religion was a powerful influence on the minds of leading thinkers. The mainland city states, often separated by mountainous terrain, were mostly independent of one another. The overseas colonies on the Aegean islands, on the Ionian coast of Asia Minor and in southern Italy and Sicily were also independent and scattered. In any individual city state, the ruling élite was relatively small and weak, even within its own small sphere. When seafaring became just as important to the economies of these cities as agriculture, new trading classes found it easy to overthrow the old landowning aristocracy. The resulting instability of Greek political life meant that citizens often found themselves debating, choosing between and intriguing about alternative forms of government. Of more importance for the development of science and philosophy was that many well-educated young aristocrats found themselves spiritually unequipped for the new commercial developments taking place in their cities. They became dissatisfied with old myths and legends and began to search for new ways of making sense of their existence. This occurred at a time when trading links made it possible to learn about the ideas and achievements of the Babylonian, Egyptian and Persian civilisations, while at about the same time traders wanting to keep accurate records had borrowed an alphabet from the Phoenicians and had begun writing. It thus became possible to develop complex trains of thought in Greek which could not easily be held in memory.

When they were in power, the aristocrats had been satisfied with a religion based on the gods of Olympus, expressed in large part through epic poetry passed down orally from the time of Homer, a legendary figure of the eighth century BC. This religion focused its followers' minds on earthly life. It emphasised the noble virtues and concerned itself with tales of high-born Greeks living honourably, often heroically, according to a god-given code. For the common people, and even for aristocratic women, religion was often very different. Dionysian cults, which sought other-worldly salvation from the desolation of this world, attracted many. Communion with the other world was to be gained mystically through physical intoxication, and the practices of these cults included many excesses.

A third religious strain, finding its typical expression in the Orphic mysteries, was a synthesis of the other two. Followers of the mythical poet and musician Orpheus sought a more refined Dionysian approach to the divine through spiritual elevation and mystical insight. The Orphic religion took root among the sons of overthrown aristocrats; so, among many of them, did the habit of philosophical and scientific inquiry as their avenue to spiritual enlightenment.

This then was the socio-religious background which gave rise to the great flowering of Greek philosophy which was to later influence not only Christian doctrine but also the work of the early Islamic scholars before undergoing revolutionary transformation in the seventeenth century. It was a period noted for its synthesis of religious inspiration and scientific inquiry, for the pervading spirit of free investigation which nurtured the interchange and development of ideas and conceptual tools which were to dominate European thought for many centuries.

A quest for unity

The earliest-known Greek philosopher was Thales (teaching about 550 BC). He was a native of Miletus on the Ionian coast, a wealthier region than the mainland, and one where the aristocracy was eclipsed by traders and merchants much earlier. Thales was considered an eccentric by his fellow townspeople because he travelled to Persia and Babylon not for trade but to seek wisdom. He is said to have styled himself a 'lover of knowledge' and seems to have wanted to develop his mind for the sake of seeking the divine. Two younger Milesians, Anaximander and Anaximenes, are said to have been his pupils. Between them, the three defined many of the questions which preoccupied later Greek philosophy. They were concerned especially with a question which became known as the problem of the One and the Many.

The Milesians speculated that the incomprehensible variety of the Many, the different substances that they could see about them, might really be just one basic substance appearing in different forms with a law-like regularity. They were stimulated in this way of thinking by observation. Thales considered that water was the basic material, because it became ice in the mountains in winter and seemed to turn into air when it boiled and into silt on the bottom of the river Maeander. Anaximenes thought that air must be the basic substance. Anaximander believed that three elements – fire, earth and water – were the essence of the visible world, and that an invisible ultimate substance united them.

The Milesian theory of the elements ranks as one of the first scientific insights, because it attempted to explain nature in terms of itself – by reducing complex phenomena in nature to the workings of simpler, more basic natural phenomena. These natural reductions were inseparable from a spiritual train of thought. The ultimate material, whether water, air or something invisible, was conceived by the Milesians to be a living god called Kosmos, who caused the Many to appear out of the One – his own substance – by divine intention.

This swift recourse to the supernatural to explain the natural was not theoretical laziness, for much mental energy and subtle thought went into a search for the rational principles on which Kosmos would construct the world. As an attempt at science it can be criticised for starting from very slender observational data and for not seeing the need to check its conclusions against experience. But complex methods have to begin somewhere, and it was perhaps not a bad first step towards developing tools of reason to ask how a being with reason would give regularity to a world.

It has been suggested that Greek learning was to remain mainly philosophical, failing to develop and deepen its scientific side, because technology in the ancient world was never sufficiently advanced to provide the precise instruments of measurement, the timepieces and the balances, that are the practical foundations of an experimental method. Perhaps more significant than this, however, is that mankind was not yet ready to ask the type of question that can be answered only by weighing substances in a balance or timing the rates of acceleration of falling bodies. There was a need first of all to discover and exercise the use of reason. As a result, an early trend in Greek philosophy was to regard the rational, unifying activity of the One as the most important object of consideration, while viewing the diversity and change observable in the Many as relatively uninteresting.

Heraclitus (teaching about 500 BC), who came from Ephesus, another Ionian city, sought to counter this trend by according the One and the Many equal importance. He taught that unity can reveal itself only through diversity, and that all diversity presupposes an underlying unity. His understanding of diversity, however, had a stronger impact on the Greek imagination than his concept of unity. For him the underlying god-like substance was fire – and, as befits the realm of a fiery god, the world is in a constant state of flux, a self-contradictory unity of opposites. For example, according to Heraclitus, you can never put your foot into the same river twice; the second time you put your foot in, the original water has moved on, and the original object has changed into something else. Plato (428–347 BC), the great Athenian synthesiser of all the main trends in Greek philosophy, was to incorporate into his system this notion that the many observable things contain their own contradiction – as, much later, did Hegel and also Hegel's most famous student, Karl Marx. But Plato was to argue that the observable world was therefore imperfectly real. For a vision of the One, he preferred Parmenides.

Parmenides (about 500–450 BC), a native of Elea in southern Italy, contributed to the further development of the Milesian theory of elements. Greek thinkers were by now counting all four: fire, earth, water and air. Parmenides also taught that change, motion and the multitude of sensible things are really just an illusion; the only real being, he said, is the One, Kosmos, infinite and indivisible. A pupil of Parmenides, Zeno of Elea (born about 490 BC), is famous for the paradoxes he proposed, to show that our conceptions of the Many and of their motion are nonsensical. The Stadium Paradox, for example, states that you cannot complete the course round a stadium, because first of all you must run half-way, but before you can do that you must run half of half-way, and so on – an infinite series of tasks.

Pythagoras (about 582–507 BC), of the Aegean island of Samos, was another major influence on Plato. Pythagoras was deeply mystical. His followers, who believed in reincarnation and a transmigration of souls towards the perfection of the one most perfect being, lived in communities according to strict religious rules. His vision of the divine, however, allowed something of the Many to pass over the divide beween the observable and the real. He was the inventor of the deductive method in mathematics and believed numbers to be the essence of reality. This insight was crucial to the development of science, but the world was not yet ready to apply mathematics to the investigation of matter. The mathematically regular, highly intelligible reality which Pythagoras glimpsed was considered until a late date to be a purely immaterial one. There were now infinitely many Ones, each with its own Many. *One* ideal of a particular geometrical figure can be constructed abstractly in precise mathematical terms; infinitely *many* physical copies of that figure can be drawn in the sand or cut out of material substances, and none of them will approximate more than imperfectly to the model. The One remains the truly important object of consideration, while the Many are relatively uninteresting.

Socrates and Plato

The most notable influence on Plato was his teacher, Socrates (about 470–399 BC), an independent and high-minded eccentric with an aristocratic and Orphic background. In philosophy Socrates was mainly concerned with ethics and politics, but he also deeply influenced his pupils' outlook on knowledge in general. He engaged in celebrated open-air dialogues in the market-places and streets of Athens, patiently exposing flaws in other men's attempts to explain the nature of temperance, courage or justice. His refutations were not accompanied by better definitions of his own, and so he made it seem that nothing of this world can be knowable or certain. The oracle at Delphi proclaimed that Socrates was the wisest man in Greece, but Socrates himself argued that, if this were true, it was because he was the only man in Greece to realise that he knew nothing. He nevertheless put faith in divine guidance, saying that a god spoke to him. The people of Athens condemned him to death for impiety and for corrupting the youth of the city with his negative talk. He was also accused of involvement in aristocratic intrigues against the democratic Athenian system of government.

Plato freely put his own positive views into his master's mouth in his voluminous 'Socratic dialogues'. One of these, called *Timaeus*, in which the philosopher fictitiously inserted dialogue with Socrates, proposed a theory of the structure of 'matter' – of a basic material that he thought all physical things are made of. Following the lead of certain Pythagorean thinkers, Plato tried to explain observable phenomena in terms of the mathematical properties of invisible particles. Plato's matter was formless in itself but was given approximate form at certain times and places as minute copies of the abstract Form of the right-angle triangle. This Platonic investigation of material nature was not meant as a contribution to knowledge. Like his master Socrates, Plato doubted that we can be sure of anything about this world. We can have only rough impressions, which he called 'beliefs'. The theory of triangular particles was put forward as 'a plausible story' about a lower realm of reality.

The higher realm of reality, the one that could be known, is glimpsed especially in Plato's Socratic dialogue *The Republic*. There, Plato has Socrates speak of a world of Forms (something like a set of ideal images stored up in the mind of God) which is independent of and more real than our sensible world. The multitude of changing, imperfect, destructible particular things which we can see, touch, hear, smell and taste in our world have only an inferior reality. They are more real than reflections in mirrors or paintings on walls, but barely real at all when compared with the Forms, which they in turn merely reflect. Knowledge of the Forms is by means of the intellect alone, and that knowledge is innate, for according to Plato we are all reincarnated transmigrating souls which have the knowledge of the Form of every kind of thing within us because we are ourselves imperfect copies of the ideal Form of human being. In Plato's ideal world, society would be ruled by philosopher kings – lovers of knowledge who have gained their regal position through the ability to free themselves of the illusion that they know the world through the senses. Liberated minds such as these, Plato reasoned, would allow dimly remembered innate knowledge to become clear and would guide the rulers towards sound judgement.

There is a profound sense of goal-directedness in Plato's vision. All things, including human beings, tend in the direction of their own best nature, towards the ideal Forms of which they are copies. But the imperfections resulting from our self-contradictory, changing and material nature make us capable of only approximating, at best, to what gives our existence its true meaning.

The atomists

A radical departure from the mainstream of Greek thought was made by the atomists, notably Democritus (about 460–370 BC), from Abdera in Thrace in northern Greece. Like many others, the atomists reasoned that physical reality can be divided into smaller-than-visible particles, and that, at the invisible level, natural phenomena might exist which could help to account for the diversity and behaviour of visible substances. Unlike Plato, they speculated that the ultimately indivisible particles into which visible elements could be divided were unchanging and everlasting. They called these particles 'atoms' and asserted that reality is composed solely of atoms (of different shapes and sizes for the different elements) and of the void through which they move without purpose, colliding, rebounding from one another and, in certain circumstances, clustering and combining in vast systems such as our universe. The name Kosmos became for the atomists a mere word, 'cosmos', referring to a universe of atoms.

To those for whom materialism is the essence of the scientific attitude, it may seem surprising that this refusal to seek a supernatural explanation for natural phenomena was not the beginning of a scientific revolution. Atomism failed for two reasons. First, it was too all-encompassing in its materialism – it confronted an audience of mainly pious Orphic seekers after wisdom with the claim that only atoms and void exist. This was not to be the view of the seventeenth-century physicists who eventually did bring about a scientific revolution, and it was enough in itself to prejudice the mainstream against taking atoms into their own view of nature even in a more moderate way. Second, it proposed no scientific method. If ever there was an area of science in which precise technology is needed before the experimental checking of theories can become possible, it is atomic theory. Theories of the invisible structure of matter did not begin to develop usefully until relatively late in our own scientific revolution, and in ancient Greece they were just one more piece of speculation.

Aristotle

Ironically, it was Plato's pupil Aristotle (384–322 BC), from Stagira in Thrace, who was to do most to prepare the way for a scientific revolution. Aristotle was a thinker of immense subtlety and breadth. Not sharing the Parmenidean rejection of a plural, changing world, he drastically revised Plato's metaphysics, making the Many into worthy objects of study. He asserted that the form of a thing has no separate existence from its realisation in particular things. He rejected any talk of invisible particles as unnecessary speculation and concentrated in his physics on questions with which the age could come to grips in at least a partially empirical way: studying what regularities there may be in the physical behaviour of observable bodies. The questions in statics and dynamics which he pioneered were to be the very starting-points of the scientific revolution of the seventeenth century. Many elements of what is today recognised as scientific method were present in his study of nature. He engaged in and encouraged in his pupils the collection of impressive bodies of data. He conducted at least some experiments, and his immediate followers conducted many.

Aristotle is remembered, however, for having a crippling effect on the development of science. This is not so much on account of his famous mistakes of observation. (He asserted that women have fewer teeth than men, for example, and he is supposed to have propounded a law that the rate of fall of a body is proportional to its weight – although this may be a misinterpretation of what he said.) Aristotle's work failed to generate a sudden leap forward in science mainly because his philosophical views did not adequately break with the mainstream of Greek thought. In particular, he did not free himself from Plato's ideas, and retained a reworked theory of the Forms.

Aristotle also retained Plato's concept of the goal-directedness of particular things towards their ideal form. He explained the behaviour of physical objects, for example, in terms of bodies behaving or approximating true to their nature. In his general theory of motion, Aristotle seems prepared to explain falling bodies simply by saying that it is a natural tendency of heavy things to go down, and of light things such as fire and smoke to move upward. 'Down' means towards the unmoving centre of the universe, the earth. Apart from the stars (thought to have no motion), the heavenly bodies are said by their nature to display circular motion around this unmoving centre.

It seemed natural, and it was in keeping with an established Greek tradition, to assume that the sun, the moon and the planets would have a special, more perfect kind of motion than earthly things, for each heavenly body is unique, a One. The Greeks thought they were observing something immaterial, something more perfectly formal and nearer to God than their own immediate world, when they gazed at the skies. There was no concept of physical forces at work in the heavens, and the very existence of motion there was taken as a proof of the existence of a god or gods.

A tension existed between this vision of perfection and some of the details of what could be more closely observed. Aristarchus of Samos (about 310–230 BC), building on the work of Heraclides of Pontus (about 388–315 BC), is reported to have suggested that the earth might be just one of the planets, revolving like each of them around the sun and rotating on its axis once in 24 hours. This model was much simpler than the earth-centred one. As developed by astronomers and finalised by Ptolemy (teaching about AD 140 in Alexandria), the earth-centred model, in order to be consistent with a growing body of observations, needed to picture planets revolving around the earth in epicycles. These were extra loops around the main circle of orbit. Antiquity preferred this complicated model for unscientific reasons – because it fitted in better with the philosophical and religious outlook of the age.

Aristotle retained the Platonic notion that matter is essentially formless, and taught that the form of a particular thing, which can still be held in the mind after the matter is ignored, is the proper object of our mental effort when we investigate the nature of physical reality. The world is to be known by means of properly exercising our intellect, not by *examining* its tangible features. Experiment and observation seem to have been used only as stimuli to theorising by Aristotle and his school in their detailed work on earthly mechanics. When empirical results conflicted with theory, this was often considered not to be surprising and was attributed to the complicating presence of matter in experimental bodies made of matter and form together. In this, the Aristotelians were no more scientific than certain followers of Plato. For example, Archimedes (about 287–212 BC), credited with being the initiator of the branch of physics called statics, applied mathematical analysis with great success to the concepts of pressure and equilibrium in liquids and to the concept of the lever. Yet he accepted a similar incompatability between theory and experience, on the grounds that the concrete objects of experiment and observation have inferior reality to the Forms, the true objects of study.

Aristotle, however, cannot be held responsible for the most negative effect of his work. Since he was the greatest philosopher and scientist of antiquity, his teachings came to dominate the ages preceding our own scientific revolution. Those ages were hungry for authority, and so Aristotle's ideas became almost as sacred as holy scripture. If a revolution has to knock a man off a pedestal in order to succeed, the man may come to seem an enemy; but, nurtured as he was in a habit of open dialogue and ever eager to improve on his own teacher's theories, it is unlikely that Aristotle would have been pleased to know that his reputation would be used in a war against free inquiry.

The Impact of Christianity and Islam

The fabric of Greek science was rent by history and passed down through the centuries as divided remnants in the hands of ancient and medieval churchmen, Islamic philosophers and the librarians of the Byzantine Empire. Threads held in all of these different hands did not finally come together again until the Renaissance. Then the Church of Rome tried to hold fast to them all to prevent a new age from adding strands of its own and weaving an entirely new cloth. Especially during the period of the Counter-Reformation, which followed the Renaissance and saw the start of the scientific revolution, there was a strong religious will to resist scientific progress. What is the background to a religion becoming such an enemy of learning and how do the non-Christian religions fit into this picture?

Greece and Rome

Greece experimented briefly with empire-building when Alexander of Macedon, whose tutor in boyhood had been Aristotle, achieved a sudden military conquest, between 331 and 323 BC, overrunning the whole of the civilised world. The Greeks were unskilled in political unification, and on Alexander's death the single empire fell into several, all with Macedonian rulers. These rulers introduced their own language and culture to the Middle East and Egypt, and Alexandria in Egypt became the most important centre of Greek learning. For many hundreds of years this language and culture were to dominate the eastern Mediterranean, but the Greek rulers themselves were soon replaced. Comparatively uncultured Romans marched in from the West to take over the function of administration.

It was not the Romans of this great age of empire who were to make Greek thought their own. They were soldiers and engineers, not given to viewing the material world, the one in which a catapult or battering-ram does its work, as being in any way less real than one merely thought of by philosophers. They admired Greek mathematics, architecture and art. They readily took to Homeric poetry and to the gods of Olympus, claiming the identity of these with their own gods. A myth developed about the first Romans being descended from refugees of the Trojan War, so that the new rulers of Greece felt a sense of participation in the heroic age of their prestigious subject people. In philosophy, they took some interest in the more practically minded and least metaphysical schools of ethics. Most of the rest they left alone.

Early Christianity

Unlike the Greeks, the Romans were skilled in political unification. Their style was often brutal and exploitative, but they believed, at least, that among their goals was the pursuit of an ideal – a unified empire for all humanity in which national divisions would be overcome for the good of all. For this reason, and because stability was considered good in itself, Roman administrators desired a uniformity of mind and of spiritual habit within their wide frontiers. Local gods were tolerated, but the Roman Empire's diverse peoples were encouraged and sometimes ordered to worship the Graeco-Roman gods as well, especially in the periods when these included the emperor himself.

It was especially difficult for one subject people, the Hebrews, to comply with this policy, because their local religion was more intrinsically bound up with their national identity than most. The Jews had a long history of resisting assimilation by their many conquerors, including Egyptians, Babylonians and Macedonians, by means of strict cultural codes and acceptance of only one God whose chosen people they believed themselves to be. Jewish determination to resist being included in one Roman world was eventually overcome by military force. Their temple in Jerusalem, a focus of national identity, was destroyed in AD 70, and most of the population was transported to scattered corners of the Empire, making it impossible for the Jews to reassert themselves as a nation.

Christianity originated in Palestine shortly before these events. It was at first perceived to be a synagogue cult, in the early years keeping the exclusively Jewish laws. However, St Paul, a partially romanised Jew who shared the Roman vision of one world with one people, conceived of the Christian mission in wider terms. He persuaded the early Christians to accept converts without requiring them to follow Jewish dietary laws and without requiring males to be circumcised. The Jewish vision of themselves as God's chosen people came to be replaced by a Christian doctrine of an elect few, drawn from all nations, who would achieve salvation. All men and women deserved damnation because of Adam's sin, but by his grace God had chosen to reveal his truth to some. Those who accepted the truth would achieve an eternal reward. Those who rejected it would remain with the damned. Spreading throughout the Empire, and maintaining its rejection of Roman gods, the new religion became a troublesome competitor for the allegiance of the single human race that Rome was trying to create. Cruel persecution did little to halt its expansion and much to win it a following. Serious failures in the Roman state's own mission – to make a stable world – did more.

Christians believed that an end to human history, a Day of Judgement, was at hand, to be preceded by Armaggedon, a final war between the forces of good and evil. When warfare almost destroyed the Roman Empire, their persecutor, during the third century AD, this belief was reinforced, and it was found credible by ever-increasing numbers of new converts. Internal corruption and rivalry between factions weakened the state, allowing Germanic tribes from the North and Persians from the East to invade and plunder Roman territory. Epidemics and fighting reduced the population of the Empire by as much as a third. Provinces not directly affected were ruined by excessive taxation to pay the costs of the conflict.

The Church and the Roman Empire

Part of the Christian heritage from the Jews was an inclination to theocracy — rule by priests. Rabbis had often been the only leaders whom the frequently conquered Jews were able to recognise as their own, and the great defenders of Jewish nationhood had been the prophets. Early Christians similarly fended for themselves, administering their own affairs through their more or less democratically elected clergy, within the hostile world that they inhabited. Several communities with their own local priests would come under the authority of an elected bishop, and eventually senior bishops emerged to administer large regions, assisted by lesser ones. The whole structure was at first a loose one, and the unity of mind and of spiritual habit which it achieved within the vast reaches of the Empire was not rigid.

There was much anxiety that this community should meet a high standard of readiness for the imminent day of judgement that Christians expected, and they found their loose unity insufficient. Arius, a Lybian bishop (about 256–336 AD), taught that Christ was a creation of God and not himself divine. Most bishops, however, preferred a tripartite vision of the divine that reflected earlier Greek religious ideas. They accorded a mystical unity to Father, Son and Holy Ghost, three persons in one sublime substance. Each side in the dispute was deeply impatient to have its view accepted by all; for history, it seemed, was about to end. There was not time for a tolerant, centuries-long quest for the truth of the matter. The Church could inherit the place God's chosen people had held in his heart only if it truly taught what God willed that the elect should understand.

Ironically, the Church became capable of imposing a more rigid unity because its theocratic tendency helped it to fill the needs of its old enemy, the Roman Empire. Roman administrators faced a difficult task in piecing the Empire back together at the end of the disastrous third century. The Emperor Constantine (AD 288–337), following his conversion to Christianity, summoned a council of bishops to Nicaea in Asia Minor, and requested them to settle the dispute between Arius and the trinitarians and to adopt one official Church doctrine. When they could not agree, he dictated the view of the trinitarian majority to them as the first official creed of the Church (the Nicene Creed) and threatened with banishment any bishop who would not accept it.

Christianity soon afterwards became the established religion of the state, under the direct control of the emperors. The bishop of Rome, the western centre of administration for the Empire, became the most important Latin-speaking prelate, and came to be known as the pope, from the Latin *papa*, which originally meant any bishop or any father. Other religious groups, especially the Jews, were officially persecuted, while Christians were now told by the state what to believe as Christians. Two old rivals for the honour of creating one human race had merged into partnership.

But the world was not ready to be one. Germanic hordes overran the whole of western Europe and North Africa in the fifth century, and the western part of the Empire formally ceased to exist in AD 476. The Empire survived in the East, speaking Greek, with its capital at Constantinople, until 1453, when it was conquered by the Ottoman Turks, and Constantinople became Istanbul. For two centuries after the fall of the West, the state religion survived in all of the Empire's former territories, even though an independent Arianism was strong at first among the various Germanic rulers of Italy, Spain and North Africa. Christians in wide regions of the Byzantine Empire became disaffected with the official Church, however, as a result of successive doctrinal disputes that were decided against their own convictions about the relationship of Christ to his divinity. This helped pave the way for their willing inclusion in the more tolerant Islamic civilisation which appeared in the seventh century and rapidly spread through most of the Middle East, northern India, North Africa and Spain. The Byzantine Empire was reduced to a small territory, in which the emperors continued to dominate the clergy, and the Church lost any authority over the faithful in Syria and Egypt.

In the fragmented Latin-speaking world, the Church was constantly engaged in political struggles. This was partly because it had territories of its own to administer (the Papal States, falsely claimed to have been bequeathed to the Bishops of Rome by the Emperor Constantine) and partly because princes ruling their own territories were eager to appoint bishops and popes after their own taste and in their own interests. These local rulers were concerned to retain their independence to govern as they pleased while controlling believed-in priestly powers thought to guarantee personal salvation. The one princely office that endured through all the centuries, however, and exercised its influence through the whole of the Latin-speaking world was that of pope, the Bishop of Rome and the ruler of the Papal States. This singularity of office helped the papacy to develop by stages into a power that no prince could dominate.

Borrowings from the Greeks

In their struggle, the popes had philosophy on their side. Shortly before the fall of the western Empire, a Nubian priest had studied in Italy and had written in Latin the first great pieces of Catholic philosophy. The Nubian was St Augustine (AD 354–430). He adapted Plotinus, an Alexandrine Greek who had brought a particularly spiritual view of Plato to Rome in the third century AD, when Romans had begun to grow weary enough of their world to turn their minds to another. Plotinus could have 'changed a few words and phrases', said St Augustine 'and become a Christian'.

St Augustine's chief disagreement with Plato was in the source of the material world's metaphysical inferiority to eternal reality. It was no longer for logical reasons that material things were not a suitable object of inquiry. The growth, decay and all too evident imperfection of things on earth were the result of the material world's corruption by the Fall of Adam. For many centuries, Christians were to contemplate the heavens for the only glimpse they thought possible of observable order and regularity. The Greek model of a system of perfectly round, immaculately pure heavenly bodies propelled in perfectly circular orbits by the activity of unresting angelic beings suited the spirit of these later times admirably. When

Armageddon brought an end to history and Christ returned to rule the world, the very substance of the world would change to something more akin to what the planets, the sun and the moon were made of.

St Augustine transformed Plato's ideal republic into the 'City of God' (the title of his great work), conceived as the society of God's elect, with a history beginning in the Genesis story of the Old Testament. The society of the elect was intertwined in the world with the City of Satan, the society of those who would be damned. The two cities were not to be finally separated until the Day of Judgement. St Augustine saw the Christian Church as embodying the City of God in the last phase of human history and saw priests in the role of the philosopher kings, the interpreters of all truth. If any secular state was to be included in the City of God, it would have to be submissive towards the Church in all matters of belief. As we will see, the consequences of this cementing of authoritative Church doctrine with Greek scientific and philosophical ideas were to reverbrate down the centuries to the present day.

The great prestige of St Augustine's philosophy gave popes the confidence to resist domination by princes and helped to create the climate of belief that made resistance successful. By the eleventh century the papacy had emerged as a strong independent force, able to prevent princes from controlling bishops and to impose celibacy on the priesthood, in order to make priests even more of a class apart. The authority of the popes became so great that the eastern Church, with its habit of obedience to the Byzantine emperor, had to break away in the schism of 1054. The imposition of authority had once again fragmented Christendom.

The Islamic civilisation

While England and France were tormented with internal disorders and factional rivalries, and the churches of Europe were racked with controversies over religious doctrines such as the legitimate use of icons, the rulers of the Islamic Empire lived in magnificent luxury in Baghdad, the cultural capital of the world. By the eighth century, as Europe languished in the Dark Ages, the Muslim Empire reached from Spain and southern France to the borders of China and India, a spectacular fusion of diverse cultures and peoples, renowned for its patronage and promotion of learning and the arts.

When Muhammad (about AD 570–632) the founder of Islam was born, however, the Arab people, though not barbarians, lacked the cultural sophistication and refinement of the Romans and Persians. They had little time for the arts or architecture which were to characterise the Islamic civilisation; poverty of environment combined with the unending struggle to survive and eke out a living left little room for such artistic expressions, other than through poetry. The introduction of Islam into that society generated a tremendous surge of creative activity within the Arab consciousness. By providing a new purpose and a new sense of direction, it knit a loose assemblage of warring, largely nomadic tribes into a unified and powerful nation. Within less than two decades, Muḥammad united nearly all Arabia into a new religious-political community, and this unity, which effectively suppressed divisive feuds among the tribes, enabled the Arabs in the twenty years following Muḥammad's death to seize the richest provinces of the Byzantine Empire. Never before or since has a prophet won so much success so quickly. Nor has the work of a single man so rapidly and radically transformed the course of world history. Through his teachings, his personal example, and the organisational framework he established for Islam, Muḥammad laid the foundations for a distinctive new way of life, which within the space of two centuries attracted the allegiance of a significant proportion of the human race and today represents the religion of about one seventh of mankind. Over the succeeding centuries, the newly formed Arab community found and developed its own cultural identity, and in bringing its various peoples and traditions together under one empire produced a melting pot of learning which was to make a major contribution to the progress of science and society.

In AD 750 the seat of government for the Muslim Empire was moved to the newly built city of Baghdad, which rapidly expanded to embrace one million inhabitants. It developed into the greatest centre of learning the world had ever witnessed, boasting a university in addition to numerous colleges and schools which attracted students, philosophers, doctors and poets from all over the known world. Greek works on philosophy, medicine and science were enthusiastically translated into Arabic, and Arab scholars led the field in mathematics, geography and medicine.

The Islamic civilisation was also distinguished by important social developments. Cordoba, in Spain, was almost as large as Baghdad, and its suburbs extended twenty-four miles along the river banks. Its streets were paved with stone and lit with lamps; there were public gardens and fountains, a plentiful water supply, sewers, public baths and a library. Most children were taught to read and write, and free schools were built for the poor. This provided a dramatic contrast with the rest of Europe, where the towns were muddy, undrained, without public water supplies or sanitation; where few people could read or write and both baths and soap were unknown. New developments also took place in the countryside, where farming and horticulture experienced great improvements through the use of irrigation and fertilisers and the production of new varieties of fruits and flowers. It seemed that almost every aspect of society and every field of learning underwent a dynamic transformation under the beneficent patronage of the Islamic Empire.

Uncorrupted by outdated philosophies and recognising no conflict between the pursuit of learning and its own teachings, Islam provided its followers with the inspiration and incentive to investigate all the fields of knowledge. In response to explicit directives from Muḥammad himself such as, 'He who leaves his home in search of knowledge, walks in the path of God' and 'Seek knowledge from the cradle to the grave', Islam brought social progress to its people and initiated dramatic developments in science. As the Islamic Empire expanded, it synthesised the sciences and arts of the non-Arab nations it conquered, and in the process rescued from near oblivion much of the learning of antiquity. Linking the past with the future, it helped pave the way for the European Renaissance.

With the ascendency of Islam the Muslim world became the centre for mathematical studies. The Muslim scientists improved on calendrical astronomy and made excellent planetary tables; they elaborated both the Aristotelian and the Ptolemic models of the universe; they imported into Europe the Indian system of numerals and invented the symbol zero, the sine function, and the algebraic methods. The Arab mathematician Alhazen, who lived in the eleventh century, made major original contributions to the field of optics and his ideas formed the foundation of perspective in the visual arts. The medical books of the eleventh century Muslim physician and philosopher Avicenna remained the standard medical text book in the Western world until the seventeenth century.

The process of transmission of Islamic science to Europe began in the eleventh century when Christianity began to win back Spain. The city of Toledo had been a major centre for Moorish learning and contained a population of Jewish scholars who possessed and understood the great writings of Islamic philosophy and had many Arabic versions of Greek texts, including some of Aristotle's. When the Christian rulers of Castile took Toledo in battle from the Moors in 1085, it became the port of entry into Christian Europe of all the arts and sciences that Muslims had brought together over the centuries. Many European scholars worked in Spain during the twelfth and thirteenth centuries translating into Latin the Arabic texts of Arab and Greek scholars. Consequently, a rich flow of Greek and Islamic thought and of Islamic and Jewish commentaries on Greek writings began to enter Europe as Latin translations. These works formed the basis on which the science of the Renaissance was built.

The rise and decline of the Church

Improved methods of agriculture in northern Europe were creating new wealth and surplus population by the Middle Ages. Religious unity in the Catholic countries was intensified as, under the leadership of the Church, these resources were directed into military crusades against Islamic rule in Jerusalem. More resources were also available for scholarship, and the first Christian scholastics appeared. These were churchmen studying Augustinian themes in a spirit of defence and clarification of the Church's perception of truth. Their activity was enriched after Toledo passed back into Christian hands, while the Crusades brought about greater contact with Constantinople, and previously unavailable texts in Greek began to be translated into Latin.

The first European universities were founded as ecclesiastical centres of learning at the end of the eleventh century, closely modelled on the earlier Islamic centres such as the University of Baghdad. Mathematics and Aristotelian science were revived.

Discussion arose over the relative merits of Plato's and Aristotle's different approaches to physics. Aristotle's overall philosophy was eventually digested into Church doctrine by St Thomas Aquinas (1225–74), who did more than any other scholastic to reinforce the Church's and medieval European society's satisfaction that Catholic teaching was rational in every one of its details. However, Aristotle's idea that the universe had always existed was rejected because it conflicted with the Biblical account of creation. In the thirteenth century the Church reached the pinnacle of its spiritual authority.

The confidence which this success generated contributed to the Church's undoing. From the fourteenth to the early sixteenth centuries an intellectual revival, the Renaissance, flourished in Italy, and occurred at later dates in other countries. Ancient literature of every type was reintroduced to a world made more literate by the invention of printing in 1437, and whose reading public by now included laymen as well as priests. Ancient literary and visual arts, both Greek and Roman, stimulated an interest in the refinement and embellishment of earthly life. A new philosophical outlook – humanism – carefully allowed itself to explore the degrees to which human existence can be found meaningful in secular terms. Wealthy secular patrons of the arts emerged, notably the Medici family of Florence, but popes, whose delight it was to make the papal possessions splendid, were also numbered among the appreciative supporters of poets, sculptors and painters. The activity of these artists was not confined to religious themes, and even their religious works did not hesitate to exult in physical beauty.

These wordly interests of the popes were often not matched by other-wordly ones. The Renaissance was a period of profound ecclesiastical corruption in Italy, for the Church did not possess a framework of ideas that could allow secular and sacred interests to be pursued together in a balanced harmony; it had always taught that the sacred and the profane are opposed. During the Renaissance, petty warfare was virtually the permanent state of relations between the various independent Italian states (including the Papal States), as princes (including popes) sought to enrich themselves and their families at the expense of anyone who could be exploited. The pope most notoriously incapable of combining a worldly outlook with his religious function was Alexander VI (pontiff from 1492 to 1503).

He and his family, the Borgias, made murder and treachery a way of life in their pursuit of power and self-gratification.

Corruption in Italy was a major contributing cause of the Protestant Reformation in the more medieval-minded northern Europe. The North recoiled from Italian worldliness and was outraged at paying tithes to Rome, out of pious duty, only to see this money impiously spent on papal palaces, the personal adornment of popes and cardinals and on military feuding. The Lutherans severed themselves from the Catholic Church in the first part of the sixteenth century, and for thirty years warfare raged in Germany between Protestant and Catholic princes. Calvinism arose in Switzerland in the 1530s and spread to France, the Netherlands and Scotland. The Church of England split from Rome in 1534 (although not for reasons of religious reform). The shock to Rome of losing half of Christendom spurred the Church into hasty self-reform in a desperate struggle to reclaim its lost spiritual authority. The Renaissance abruptly ended in Italy. The popes became pious once more, and the Inquisition, a general tribunal established in 1233 for the discovery and punishment of heretics, was given renewed impetus to pursue its work of obtaining conformity with the Church's doctrines wherever it could lay its hands on dissenters.

This, then, was the atmosphere in which energies unleashed in the Renaissance were to emerge in the work of Galileo. A Hebrew tradition of rule by priests offering salvation to the faithful had been transferred to Europe, partly with the help of a Roman emperor recently converted to the Christian Faith. Greek philosophy had also been grafted on to Christianity, and the physical world, except for the perfectly ordered heavens, was officially viewed as being made out of a formless substance: Aristotelian 'matter'. Theocratic tradition had readily absorbed Plato's view that government would be best in the hands of a few clear visionaries who had disentangled themselves from the seductions of the material world.

The harshness of Christianity's early treatment by the Roman Empire and the expectation of an imminent end to history had done much to blind Christians to the spirit of change and development in Christ's own teachings. A mood had prevailed among the early Christians that reflected instead the rigidity of the most severe of the

Old Testament prophets; a once-and-for-all set of truths had to be taught by the new Church, or else it would fail in its claim to be the new City of God, the true people of the prophets. During long centuries, this mood prevailed. When the Renaissance allowed a more relaxed atmosphere, precisely the sort of disasters struck that an Old Testament prophet would have feared. The Church hastened to turn itself and its people back to more purely other-worldly concerns and to tighten its control over the minds of Christians. Although attempts to impose unity of thought through the doctrinal decrees of central authority had repeatedly split and fragmented Christendom, it was to this old, rigid model of unity that Rome instinctively turned in its crisis.

From the Renaissance to the Modern World

The mood of the Counter-Reformation was stern, but it could not undo the previous age. A spirit of rediscovery, not of invention, had marked the Renaissance, but new ideas had nevertheless crept into the world and were not to be dislodged. One aspect of the intensification of scientific activity was a renewed interest in collecting data and making observations. In addition, the rediscovery of disagreement between the ancients, by a much wider society than had been aware of it during the Middle Ages, made literate people expect to have alternatives to entertain, at least hypothetically, while persuading themselves of the official view of reality. New observations eventually began to put an increasing strain on old models, and some of the alternatives took a powerful hold on thoughtful minds. At the same time, a novel way of thinking about material things had been taking root among rising classes of writers who were not properly educated in the old philosophy. It was a way of thinking that would lead at last to a scientific method of investigation. The method was to emerge in the laboratories of post-Renaissance thinkers like Galileo, who launched the world into its modern era.

Artists and engineers
One of the earliest and most marked Renaissance innovations, largely inspired by Islamic artists and mathematicians, was the introduction of a three-dimensional perspective into drawing and painting, as

artists pursued an ever more convincing naturalism. It must have been evident to educated people that this encouraged the glorification of material reality in a way that Plato (who had banished all poets, artists and other illusionists from his ideal republic) could never have approved. It was probably less obvious that treatises by these newly literate artists were quietly undermining the very concepts of the Church's approved philosophers. Renaissance writings on perspective and spatial harmony employed the tools of mathematics, and these tools were used to describe not ideal geometrical objects but the material world that artists intended their illusions to represent. Niceties such as the Aristotelian wisdom that physical things are made of a formless substance that is in itself without mathematical properties, and the Platonic view that the material world has only approximate mathematical regularity, were not taken into account.

Another rising class of Renaissance innovators was the engineer. His new-found literacy enabled him to study mathematics and physics and to apply his learning to the geometrical arrangement of gun emplacements in war or to the improvement of machinery. The new scientific approaches to art and engineering were brilliantly combined in Leonardo da Vinci (1452–1519). His paintings and drawings are considered works of outstanding genius, but he also served as a military engineer to the infamous Caesar Borgia, and he left notebooks on problems in hydraulics and mechanics. Many engineers who attempted to write on such topics revealed a major gap in their understanding of Greek physics. With a typical Renaissance bow to ancient authority, they claimed that they were heirs to Archimedes, a Platonist, in applying mathematical principles to the behaviour of material things. In saying this they failed to grasp that Archimedes observed the behaviour of material levers and material water only to give him an insight into the Forms which he took them to reflect. Interested primarily in making machines work, Renaissance engineers did not go into such refinements, and they assumed that if their machines did not work the fault lay with their own understanding of mathematics and physics, not with the metaphysical inferiority of matter. The machines that they constructed were to become the model for a new conception of material nature in the seventeenth century, when the entire universe came to be seen as an immensely grander version of that Renaissance invention, the chiming clock.

Astronomical challenges

The Renaissance man most noted for hastening the onset of the scientific revolution, however, was a more sophisticated individual, a Polish pure mathematician who was a devotee of Plato, whom he considered superior to Aristotle. Out of a Platonic admiration for abstract simplicity and beauty, Nicolas Copernicus (1473–1543) calculated a precise model of the planetary motions as Aristarchus is reported to have envisaged them in ancient times: with the sun at their centre, the earth revolving around it with them and rotating daily on its axis.

Copernicus published this work only in the year of his death, and then with a careful explanation that it was to be understood as a mathematical exercise only. Gradually, however, as it became clear that this model accorded better with observation than Ptolemy's, it acquired a more profound significance than its author had been bold enough to claim for it. New astronomical observations lent it increasing support, particularly those of Tycho Brahe (1546–1601), a Dane who used improved astronomical instruments (but not yet the telescope) and pin-pointed the changing positions of heavenly bodies.

Brahe's own proposed planetary system, a compromise between Ptolemy and Copernicus, was not put forward as a mere intellectual exercise but as the best interpretation he could offer of what he had actually seen. His observations transformed the Copernican thought experiment into the Copernican revolution: an overturning of belief. They also broadened the scope of the revolution. By recording the passage of a distant comet, Brahe undermined the traditional view that comets are confined to the earth's atmosphere. They had been thought too transitory, their appearance too sporadic and their motion too erratic to belong to the heavenly regions of perfect motion and immaculate form. (St Augustine had accounted for the erratic movements of comets by supposing them to be manifestations of angels carrying out divinely appointed tasks.) Brahe also recorded a new star, implying the possibility of growth and decay in the most outward sector of the heavens, hitherto assumed to be an unchanging spectacle of everlasting stellar pefection.

In religiously disrupted, newly Protestant Denmark, where the theocratic tendency in Christianity had not been able to reassert itself, Brahe had the freedom to comment on the results of his star-gazing. In Catholic countries, however, the Church considered itself in charge of all learning and investigation. There was a clear message for all in its reaction to Giordanno Bruno (1548–1600), an Italian monk who vigorously rejected the cosmology of the day. He developed a medieval conception of physical 'minima' into a picture similar to that of the Greek atomists: invisibly small particles came together in the void to form an infinite plurality of worlds; not only did the earth move around the sun, but the sun moved, and it was just one of countless swarming stars, each the centre of its own system. For his militant unorthodoxy Bruno was burnt at the stake in Rome in 1600. The revolutionary century was dawning.

Galileo

Galileo Galilei (1564–1642), a teacher of physics at the University of Padua, was the next Catholic scientist to find himself in conflict with the Inquisition. Hearing reports of the telescope invented in Holland, he made one for himself in 1609 and turned it on the heavens. Sun-spots and craters of the moon appeared in his lens, revealing a far from unblemished character in the celestial bodies. The phases of Venus – the changes in its pattern of illumination by the sun – were as the Copernican, rather than earth-centred, model would predict. Jupiter was discovered to have four moons. When Galileo reported these observations to the professors of philosophy at the university the learned men were convinced that they must be artefacts. Rather than bringing the heavens into better view, the telescope must be distorting them in some way. Among their arguments was that Jupiter's four moons would bring the number of heavenly bodies to eleven, not the traditional seven: five known planets, the sun and the moon. Eleven was a number not traditionally recognised as having mystical properties, but seven was – for the sabbath is the seventh day. It was not credible that the perfect way in which the heavens had always been understood to reflect this number should be overturned by mere human observation.

Galileo persisted in claiming that the empirical evidence for the Copernican model should be heeded. He was summoned in 1616 to Rome, where the highest authorities in the Church ardently believed that he was allowing himself to be used as a tool of Satan. By creating the illusion of a moving world, just one of many planets of a distant sun, an evil influence was trying to separate God's elect from a centuries-old understanding of the moral and historical significance of their material nature: created in God's own image in a Garden of Eden which was the pinnacle of creation, at the very centre of the universe, humanity had corrupted itself and the world by a wicked misuse of its free will. If any were now to be saved from the consequent damnation, it was because the Church had divine authority and a mission. In private sitting, the Inquisition condemned Galileo's view as heretical and obliged him to renounce his support for the new astronomy.

In 1623 Cardinal Barberini, a friend of Galileo's, became Pope Urban VIII. This gave Galileo a new sense of security and prompted him to start writing his *Dialogues on the Two Great Systems of the World,* which was published in 1632. This work contained all of his arguments in favour of the Copernican system and was widely read in Europe. Once again, he was summoned to Rome. He arrived there in 1633, an old man of sixty-nine. His one-time friend Pope Urban VIII, now turned bitter enemy, allowed Galileo to be thrown into the prisons of the Inquisition and threatened with tortue if he did not recant. When he did recant, he was at first condemned to prison, and later forced to live in closely monitored solitude, forbidden to see even his family. Galileo became blind in 1637 and died in 1642, the year that Newton was born.

These public events had a wide following and did much more to harm the authority of the Church than to reinforce it. The attention of wide sections of society was drawn to the controversy and to the Copernican way of thinking. Galileo's conscientious commitment to the pursuit of truth was an example which inspired many. His defence implied a strong criticism of the Church's use of its authority, but not of religion. It can be summarised in his famous dictum: 'The Bible tells us how to go to heaven but not how the heavens go.'[1] His faith in scientific observation and his religious faith went side by side. Indeed, he considered himself a good

Catholic who was critical only of abject submission to tradition and excessively literal interpretations of the Bible. In his *Letter to the Grand Duchess Cristina,* written in 1615 and published in 1636, he said:

> I think in the first place, that it is very pious to say and prudent to affirm that the Holy Bible can never speak untruth — whenever its true meaning is understood. But I believe that nobody will deny that it is often very abstruse, and may say things which are quite different from what its bare words signify.[2]

In the same letter Galileo expressed the belief that his faith in God did not require him to deny reason:

> I do not feel obliged to believe that the same God who has endowed us with senses, reason and intellect has intended to forego their use and by some other means to give us knowledge which we can attain by them. He would not require us to deny sense and reason in physical matters which are set before our eyes and minds by direct experience or necessary demonstrations.[3]

Galileo is considered the founder of modern science, not on account of his conflicts with the Church, and not merely for looking through a telescope. He initiated a true revolution in scientific method. Heir to the Renaissance engineer's way of thinking, and himself a part-time military engineer in the employ of the Duke of Tuscany, he formulated a new definition of 'matter' to replace Aristotle's, and he provided science with the method to investigate it. Newton, the father of modern physics, was to build all of his foundations on Galileo's mechanics.

Aristotle had defined matter in an extremely abstract manner as that which was left when all of the properties of a thing (its colour, taste, shape, weight, etc.) were subtracted from the idea of that thing; matter was in itself a featureless substance which properties inhabited, something like overnight guests. For Galileo, the notion of matter continued to be abstract, but he subtracted much less from a physical object before arriving at its matter. In *The Assayer* (1623) he divided properties into primary and secondary. The secondary properties include all that we perceive in an object by sensation: colour, taste, an impression of heaviness or lightness, etc. These properties, he thought, were subjective; they did not really exist in the object and were perceived by the human mind only as a result of primary properties of the object acting upon our sense organs. The primary properties included all those which belong 'objectively' to the object, and Galileo thought of these as the properties that can be measured according to *standards* of measurement, the weight of the object and its dimensions, for example, or the velocity at which it is travelling. Primary properties also included objective properties which had not yet been discovered and those that science had not yet learned how to measure, including properties of the atoms that Galileo suspected matter to be made of, and the properties that cause our subjective sensations of colour, taste, etc. The more properties of material things we learn to measure, and the more predictions that we learn to calculate mathematically on the basis of these properties, thought Galileo, the more we learn about matter itself.

This distinction between primary and secondary properties was echoed in the greatest philosophical works of the seventeenth century – Descartes's *Meditations* and Locke's *Essay Concerning Human Understanding*. It has met with serious objections from present-day philosophers, but the importance of Galileo's definition of matter does not lie in its being philosophically the last word on the subject. What is important is the power it was able to exert on the seventeenth-century mind. Aristotle's conception of matter was of something incapable of having mathematical properties in itself. Plato's was of something at best having only a rough, borrowed mathematical regularity. These conceptions were now overthrown by a view of matter as essentially mathematical, i.e. highly struct- ured and regular. Galileo left no room for a gap between truth in physics and the way material objects behave. Either the mathematic- ally calculated predictions of a theory were consistent with observa- tions, or the theory was false.

Galileo's *Discourses and Demonstrations Concerning Two New Sciences*, published in 1638, is a treasure-house of new physical concepts constructed with calculation and experiment in mind. It introduces the concept of moment, the turning action of a force about a ful- crum, to the theory of machines. Without this idea, the formulation of a quantified concept of the work done by such a force had been impossible. The book introduces to physics the concepts of internal strains and breaking stresses in loaded beams. It discusses the possibility of measuring nature's resistance to the formation of a vacuum. Its greatest contributions, however, are in dynamics, the science of bodies in motion, virtually founded by Galileo in its post-Aristotelian form.

It had been argued that if the earth was in motion, falling through space in orbit around the sun, it would fall much more quickly than all of the small unattached objects and creatures we see every day resting securely on its surface. According to the standard interpretation of Aristotle, the rate at which a body falls is a function of its weight; so all of these lighter bodies should be left behind. Galileo refuted this argument with simple experiments. He timed spheres of different weights as they rolled own an inclined plane (and many also have dropped leaden balls from the Leaning Tower of Pisa, although that is probably only a story). After taking into account differences due to the resistance of the air through which the spheres moved, he was able to claim empirical backing for the principle that all bodies, regardless of weight, fall at the same rate through a vacuum; even a feather in a vacuum would fall like a dead weight.

He also demonstrated that the rate of fall in a body is not constant. He timed his spheres at different points in their path and showed that they continuously accelerated; a falling body's velocity is proportional not to its weight but to the time spent falling. This sharp distinction between velocity (rate of motion) and acceleration (increase in velocity) allowed Galileo to ask a searching question: does the continuing incline of the plane explain both the continuation of the motion and the acceleration or does it explain only the acceleration? He went on to demonstrate that a ball rolling from an inclined plane to a horizontal one would, but for resistance, continue rolling without any increase or decrease in its velocity for as long as it continued on the horizontal plane. It is the resistance of the horizontal surface, not any innate tendency in the sphere, which slows the sphere down and stops it. This introduction of a natural tendency to keep moving represented an important break with Aristotelian physics, which had taught that only a tendency towards rest is natural in earthly mechanics. Galileo set the modern age on the path towards an understanding of inertia.

His own understanding of inertia was not to be Newton's, for

Galileo thought that the natural direction of inertial motion is in a circle. He conceived of his horizontal plane not as a straight line but as one following the curvature of the earth's surface. If it were not for resistance, the experimental sphere would travel without change of velocity around the world again and again on a single path. Although this contradicted Aristotle's earthly physics, it allowed Galileo to explain to his own satisfaction the motions of the planets in a modified Aristotelian way; the earth, the other planets and everything on them move in circular orbits around the sun at fixed velocities simply by inertia, by a natural tendency to move in their circular paths.

Another tenet of Aristotelian physics to be overthrown by Galileo was the assertion that contrary motions cannot occur simultaneously in the same object. This teaching had encouraged people to think that a cannon ball fired horizontally travels horizontally then suddenly falls vertically to its destination. In the same manner of thinking, Aristotelians wondered how it can be possible, if the earth rotates, to throw a ball straight up and see it land almost at the point where it started. Why is it not left behind by the moving earth, to land a few paces away from the starting-point? Sympathisers with the Copernican view had suggested that perhaps the air carries the ball along in some way, but Galileo explained this phenomenon by showing that the ball exhibits simultaneous motions: *down* towards the earth, and *horizontally* along with the earth. If a rolling sphere moving at a constant rate along a horizontal table is allowed to drop over the edge, nothing prevents its continued horizontal motion, but vertical motion is now added to it, and the two together cause the sphere's path to follow a parabolic curve. Similarly, a weight dropped from the mast of a moving ship will continue to move horizontally with the ship at the same time as falling down. It will only seem to fall vertically.

Descartes
Another contributor to the new science to consider himself a good Catholic was the great French philosopher René Descartes (1591–1650), who chose to live in Protestant Holland. There he received the protection of the Duke of Orange, who was not swayed by his Protestant scholars when they became alarmed at Descartes's

rejection of Aristotelian orthodoxy. Nevertheless, Descartes did not want to be excommunicated by the Catholic Church, and after Galileo's condemnation by the Inquisition in 1634 he deliberately withheld from publication his treatise *Le Monde*. This work accepted the Copernican view and offered a complete theory of the origins and workings of the solar system in terms of mathematical laws and quantifiable sizes, shapes and motions of 'gross' particles of matter carried in an ether composed of particles of 'subtle' matter. When at last he published his scientific views in 1644, he cautiously put forward the Copernican model as an assumption for purposes of discussion rather than as a piece of scientific truth.

Descartes is remembered mainly as a philosopher and a mathematician (the inventor of co-ordinate geometry). Most of his scientific views were swept aside by Newton, and he did not contribute significantly to experimental science. Some of his most important models did not in fact produce easily quantifiable concepts – his explanation of celestial motions, for example, is that the planets are carried around in a vortex of subtle matter in the way that a leaf is carried around in a whirlpool. His importance for the history of science lies rather in the wide dissemination of his sweepingly materialistic view of nature. Attempts to prove by logic that God exists were central to his overall system of knowledge, but in the end he effectively relegated God to the role of a distant and strangely impersonal creator of a vast, self-running machine. Even animals and humans are machines, with the difference that the human machine has an immaterial soul attached, working it somehow through impulses of will communicated mechanically to the brain through a pineal gland. It is a short step from the devout Descartes to a totally materialist view of reality.

Newton

Lasting progress towards understanding the details of material reality was to receive greater impetus from thinkers who were less concerned with first principles and more interested in explaining particular observations. There was, for example, Johannes Kepler (1571–1630). In 1609 Kepler published in his *New Astronomy with Commentaries on the Motions of Mars* two laws of planetary motion which Galileo rejected, but which gained a wide hearing because they were based on Brahe's detailed observations. Kepler's first law states that the path of a planet revolving around the sun must form not a circle but an ellipse, with the sun as a focal point. By accepting this form of orbit, it was possible to dispense with Ptolemy's epicycles, on which the Copernican system of circular orbits had continued to rely in part. Kepler's second law is that a planet does not revolve with uniform velocity but speeds up as it reaches the part of its elliptical path of orbit which is nearest the sun and slows down when it is farthest away. Galileo rejected these laws because he thought that inertia alone (a concept he knew Kepler did not understand) should be allowed to explain planetary motions. It was not plausible to see the direction of inertial motion as elliptical, nor to see it speeding up and slowing down.

These conflicting views were to be reconciled by Sir Isaac Newton (1642–1727), whose *Mathematical Principles of Natural Philosophy* in 1687 reworked Galileo's mechanics and added to them a mathematical conception of universal gravitation. Newton adhered to the Unitarian religious movement, which was committed to adopting no dogmas and to encouraging independent judgement and the use of reason in religious questions. He studied and taught at the University of Cambridge in an age when the Church of England had not yet secured the banishment of Nonconformists from academic institutions. A later English Unitarian, Joseph Priestly, was forced to live his scientific life outside the universities, but Newton was one of the first scientists to be completely unencumbered by religious interference with his work. Like that of Descartes, Newton's universe is easy to picture as a vast machine that God has created and then stood back from, the way a clockmaker stands back and watches his finished product work. Unlike Descartes, Newton did not make the relationship of God to his creation one of his subjects of inquiry, but instead concentrated more completely on the movement of material things through space.

With two modifications Galileo's inertial law became Newton's first law of motion: every body continues in its state of rest, or of uniform motion in a straight line, unless it is compelled to change that state by forces impressed upon it. This law extends the concept of inertia to bodies at rest and changes the direction of inertial motion from circular to straight.

Newton's Second law of motion is that change of motion is proportional to the force impressed, and it is made in the direction of the straight line in which the force is impressed. The second part of this law captures Galileo's insight into simultaneous motions: when a change occurs, it occurs in the direction given by the force; motion in any other direction neither increases nor decreases. The first part of the law says that the cause of acceleration is a force, and the greater the force the greater the acceleration.

Newton introduced a new concept – that of mass – to further clarify the idea of inertia. A body's mass is its quantified resistance to being set in motion and accelerated, similarly its resistance to being changed from an acquired direction and velocity of motion. Newton saw each body's mass as constant. (It is different from the body's weight, which depends on how much force of gravity is being exerted on the object in the place where the weighing takes place – a man on the moon weighs less than he does on earth.)

Newton's second law makes it possible to measure force, acceleration and mass in terms of one another. If the mass of a body is known, and also its rate of acceleration, then it can be calculated how much force is being exerted upon it.

The force which moved Galileo's rolling spheres down his inclined plane was gravity. In thinking of gravity as a force, Galileo and Newton were changing the meaning of this term, which in everyday usage meant 'heaviness', something in the object itself. Much opposition had to be overcome before this new usage could be understood and accepted. Not only was there the Aristotelian prejudice that objects fall because of a natural tendency within them; there was also the anxiety of the new age not to become involved with unobservable 'occult' influences. Descartes had excluded forces entirely from his theories. During the course of the seventeenth century, however, various other writers had suggested that gravity was a force of mutual attraction which bodies exerted on each other.

Newton was an advocate of the mutual attraction theory, which he combined with his mechanics to provide a model of the solar system and of the universe that was to receive hardly any revision for over two hundred years. The earth and a falling body, like any two bodies, mutually attract. The force that attracts them can be mathematically calculated as a relation between their two masses and the distance between them. This force draws the falling body, which has less resistance to acceleration, less mass, towards the greater earth. The principle is true as well of the earth and the moon, or of the sun and a planet, except that a satellite does not collide with its greater partner; there is a previously established motion at right angles to the attractive forces. Instead of falling into the sun, the planet follows an elliptical orbit, accelerating more quickly towards the sun as it sweeps closer, slowing down in its rate of fall as its momentum carries it farther away.

Newton was able to test this model empirically by comparing the motion of the moon with the motion of a falling object on earth. The moon's velocity being known, Newton calculated how far the moon would travel in one second. He also calculated the point that it would reach if it left its orbit and travelled the same distance in a straight line. The distance between this point and the point it would reach staying in orbit can be counted as the distance by which the moon falls towards the earth in one second. This figure allowed Newton to calculat the rate of acceleration of the moon towards the earth, and to demonstrate mathematically that this rate of acceleration is what it should be, compared with the rate of acceleration in a falling object on earth, if the two are indeed in the grip of the same force.

The enormous scope and predictive power of the Newtonian system made it a conceptual framework such as the world had never seen before. Confirmed many thousands upon thousands of times over by the observable occurrence of phenomena, which calculation shows should occur if the system is sound, this theory deepened immeasurably the human understanding of physical reality. It was so successful and so difficult to improve upon that Newton was for a long time in danger of becoming another Aristotle, another unintending obstacle to human development.

Scientific Method and Religious Insight

The seventeenth century gave us a more sophisticated picture of the universe than mankind had ever had before, a picture that established itself in spite of determined opposition from religious institutions. This opposition arose because the priests had a different picture to reveal to the faithful, one that they believed Christians had to believe for the sake of their souls. In the end, Christian doctrine in astronomy was overthrown, and the Church gradually revised its notions of what Christians have to believe.

New science vs old religion

Yet the main effect of the scientific revolution was something much more important than a new theory, even granting the splendour of Newton's physics. A method of inquiry became established which was to bring a previously unimaginable wealth of knowledge and benefit, together with frightening new responsibilities, as field after field of science built testable theory upon testable theory, and nature was placed under human control.

Islamic and then European alchemists had for many centuries tried to change base metals into precious ones by searching through trial and error for a way of transferring the Aristotelian 'form' of one element to the Aristotelian 'matter' of another. After the seventeenth century this hopeless enterprise was abandoned — the use of testable hypotheses diverted alchemists' laboratories and equipment into the new discipline of chemistry. Old speculations about an atomic structure in matter took a more quantifiable form as the English chemist John Dalton (1766–1844) prepared the first table of atomic weights. Physics in the nineteenth century extended the Newtonian approach to thermodynamics, hydrodynamics and the science of elastic bodies, with great success. The properties of gases came to be explained through mechanical models of collisions between molecules. The understanding of magnetism and electricity was advanced through the work of Faraday (1791–1867). It took a further step forward with the work of James Clerk Maxwell (1831–79), who predicted the discovery of electromagnetic waves. Using mathematical deduction and experimental techniques, physicists of the late nineteenth and early twentieth centuries began to penetrate the subatomic structure of matter. Albert Einstein (1879–1955) propounded his general theory of relativity, superseding Newton's theory of gravitation and drastically altering our conception of astronomical reality. From the tiniest particle to the greatest of the heavenly bodies, scientists have made progressively more sense of a world thought by the ancients to lack any true sense.

Before the scientific revolution, medicine had often been a useful herbal lore, but often too it attempted to put into practice unfounded and incoherent theories. Disease was supposed to be the work of evil spirits and demons, a belief that was supported by literal interpretations of Scripture. Plagues were attributed to God's wrath, and one method of attempting to appease this wrath was persecution of the Jews. Anatomy was considered wicked, since dissection was thought to interefere with the resurrection of the body. Jewish medical practitioners, deriving their knowledge from the medicine of the Islamic civilisation, were suspected of magic and sorcery. Barbaric treatment of mental disorders was justified on readings from the New Testament, insanity being seen as possession by evil spirits. One technique for driving out the evil spirit was to torture and humiliate it, by torturing and humiliating the sufferer.

As the scientific revolution progressed, medicine was able not only to apply the results of the scientific activity of other disciplines, but also to use its own experimental methods in the search for the causes of disease and its treatment. The Church only gradually accepted these gifts of science. Large sections of the Catholic population at first refused innoculations against smallpox, following the counsel of their clergy. There was even a theological objection to the use of anaesthetics at childbirth. Genesis iii:16 says: 'In sorrow shalt thou bring forth children.' How can a woman be in sorrow if she is under the influence of chloroform?

Technology and engineering have made the world immeasurably wealthier by applying scientific methods to its problems. Studies in heat phenomena made possible the invention of the first practical steam-engine in 1769, giving power to the Industrial Revolution. In the nineteenth century Faraday's laws of electricity and magnetism led to the development of electric telegraphy, electric motors and the generators that today make cheap power available to industry and the home. Inspired by the experimental confirmation of electro-magnetic waves by Herz, Marconi transmitted the first radio signal across the Atlantic in 1901. Greater understanding of thermo-dynamics resulted in the internal combustion and diesel engines, Daimler began making motor cars in 1887 and the Wright brothers flew in 1912.

The authority of science, first established on the theoretical level, was eventually vindicated by its practical success both in providing plausible explanations of nature and in advancing material civilisation in such fields as industry, agriculture and medicine. To the average person, it was the dramatic impact of science on everyday life that did much to win his or her support, and the prestige of science grew at the expense of theology. In the twentieth century science has become the single most dominant force in society. The traditional subjects of chemistry, mathematics and physics have cross-fertilised to produce completely new disciplines, such as cybernetics, biophysics and information technology. The economic and military strength of any nation now depends on its scientific expertise. Twentieth-century science has introduced the nuclear age, high-speed travel and instant communications. Ready or not, the world has become physically one.

For religion as well, the consequences of the scientific revolution go far beyond one defeat in an argument about astronomy. What was gradually surrendered by the priests in the end was the cardinal principle that scientists should not compete with them for authority in questions of belief. Their attempts to prevent science from emerging as an autonomous way to knowledge failed. The time has now come in our discussion to consider whether this failure truly amounts to the worst fears of those priests; does the way now stand open for science to supplant religion completely? To many it seems that this would be a just outcome of the struggle – because science has a method and religion, it seems, has none.

Scientific method

Scientific method can be summarised as consisting of three stages of investigation:

1 the careful collection and examination of all observable data relevant to the problem under investigation;
2 the formulation of a hypothesis to explain the data;
3 testing the hypothesis by experiment and observation.

It is possible to collect and examine data out of sheer curiosity. This seems to have been the spirit of much ancient and Renaissance interest in learning new facts – data collecting tended to focus on distant lands and the exotic beasts and plants that could be brought home from them by travellers. Another possibility is to collect data simply with the motive of finding persuasive evidence for a particular position, as, for example, when defence counsel sift selectively through legal evidence with an eye to what will show a client in a favourable light. In the true spirit of scientific inquiry, however, data are collected with the expectation that they will require explanation and that explaining new data may require a revision of even well-loved and admired old theories.

In proposing a hypothesis, the investigator attempts to draw from his imagination an insight into the problem that will explain why the data are as we find them. The insight is typically reductive in character, and this is a point of continuity between ancient and modern science. Since early times, there have been thinkers who have attempted to make the enormous complexity of the physical world easier to understand by redescribing the world in terms of (reducing it to) a model. The incomprehensible variety of different substances was seen by the Milesians as resulting from different combinations of a few basic elements; the elements in turn were seen by Democritus as divisible into atoms, whose 'shapes' govern the way that any one element can combine with others to form more complex substances. In modern practice, we can never put a reductive insight forward as a *scientific* hypothesis unless it is possible to conceive how its truth could be tested by quantifiable observations. Thus, theories of elements and atoms began to take on a modern form only when technology supplied the necessary means to test them. What is required is that we have the capacity to determine by mathematical calculation what consequence we should expect, what measurable results should be obtainable by experiments, as a consequence of assuming a hypothesis to be true.

The testing of hypotheses often involves exhaustive and sometimes tedious years of observation and experiment, in which scientists painstakingly measure the results of specially designed experiments, patiently looking for results disproving their own expectations. They look for calculable consequences that do not occur, for predictions that do not come true. Only when the predictions do come true, when the tests fail to disprove it, can a hypothesis achieve general acceptance as a theory. If two or more theories are equally compatible with the data, and stand up equally well to tests, then acceptance tends to go to the one that explains the widest range of data, in the simplest and most eloquent way.

Often the ability to account for the data of observation is all that recommends a theory to science. The data of astronomical observation made Ptolemy introduce complicated epicycles into the orbits of the planets in order to maintain the model of a planetary system with circular orbits and the earth at its centre. He was being unscientific; this was not a better way of accounting for the data, only a devotedly geocentric way. When Brahe's observations led Kepler to prefer elliptical orbits to circular orbits with epicycles, the spirit of science was reasserting itself.

In the same spirit as its constant readiness to record and take seriously new data, it is an ideal of science to be informed about theoretical controversies, to understand and give fair judgement on competing models as they arise out of the investigation of data, and to remain open to revisions of scientific orthodoxy. Scientists with new ideas have often experienced difficulty in winning recognition for them from conservative colleagues. Yet profound change and development, even if each stage does not come overnight, are characteristic of this constantly improving, self-critical discipline. It offers us an ever-changing and ever-deepening understanding.

Religious inquiry

Religions seem rigid by comparison, characteristically bundling beliefs in all-or-nothing parcels to be accepted on authority. In striking contrast to science's commitment to self-criticism and progress, many institutionalised religions invest considerable time and effort in maintaining official doctrine, and defending it at all costs. It seems that religious dogmas lack any rational basis and their advocates fear they are more likely to be wholly overturned than to be improved upon if there is any straying from them. "Blessed are those who believe but do not see" has been widely understood within Christianity to infer the superiority of blind faith. Consequently, new ideas and the views of other religions are systematically ignored, and religious inquiry is generally regarded as neither positive nor essential. On the contrary, followers of particular religious sects are discouraged from investigating or learning from any other sect or religion. Alternative religions, far from being seen as sources of different perspectives and new insights, capable of providing valid interpretations of religious questions and other ways of understanding God, are usually perceived as wrong or misguided, and therefore totally invalid. Frequently described as perversions of the truth, they are viewed with great suspicion due to their potential for confusing and misleading the true believer. The investigation of both one's own and other religions is not merely considered a threat to the true religion, but is often presented as a practice which leaves followers vulnerable to the attacks of Satan or evil forces, which are ever ready to lead them astray from the right path to eternal damnation.

By the turn of the century science rather than religion had come to represent the spirit of the age. Influenced by the scientists' intolerance of religion, twentieth-century society has adopted a highly critical stance, and in the eyes of the majority religion has now been reduced to a set of irrelevant dogmas and superstitions. The conflicts which raged between science and the Christian Church from the sixteenth to the nineteenth centuries lent added weight to the scientists' view of religion, particularly institutionalised religion, as typically possessing such features as: rigid dogmas incapable of changing with a progressing society; holding a set of exclusive truths which are not open to debate but are nevertheless regarded as applicable to everybody; having philosophies which are essentially selfish (such as individual salvation) and being consistently and even intrinsically opposed to science and scientific method. A few quotations from a recent book on this subject[4] are sufficient to illustrate some of the current, and very popular, objections to religion today.

More relevant to the decline of religion is the fact that science, through technology, has altered our lives so radically that the traditional religions may appear to lack the immediacy necessary to provide any real assistance in coping with contemporary personal and social problems. If the Church is largely ignored today it is not because science has won its age-old battle with religion, but because it has so radically reoriented our society that the biblical perspective of the world now seems largely irrelevant.

To argue whether the date of Creation was 4004 BC or 10,000 BC is irrelevant if scientific measurements reveal a 4.5 billion-year-old Earth. No religion that bases its beliefs on demonstrably incorrect assumptions can expect to survive very long.

Few would deny that religion remains, for all its pretentions, one of the most divisive forces in society. Whatever the good intentions of the faithful, the bloodstained history of religious conflict provides little evidence for universal standards of human morality among the major organized religions. Nor is there any reason to believe that love and consideration are lacking in those who do not belong to such organizations, or even committed aetheists.

In contrast, religion is founded on revelation and received wisdom. Religious dogma that claims to contain unalterable Truth can hardly be modified to fit changing ideas. The true believer must stand by his faith whatever the apparent evidence against it. This 'Truth' is said to be communicated directly to the believer, rather than through the filtering and refining process of collective investigation. The trouble about revealed 'Truth' is that it is liable to be wrong, and even if it is right other people require a good reason to share the recipients' belief.

It is clear from the above that many of the most commonly encountered objections to religion are in fact reactions to the dogmatic and fanatical elements that have been present to varying degrees in the Christian Church over many centuries. Is the generalisation that all religions intrinsically behave like the Christian Church fair? In fact, do the Christian Churches really represent true Christianity?

20th century scientific dogma
Today's society views science and religion as totally incompatible. While it may be true that the conflict between them was largely caused by representatives of religion in the past, in the twentieth century the blame for their continued deadlock may be laid at the door of those who claim to follow science. One could argue that

there are implicit misconceptions in science today which prevent it from considering the possibility that science and religion could be in harmony. These prejudices are religiously and almost universally held not only by the international scientific community but by society at large, and it is to these prejudices that we should now turn our attention.

Foremost among these dogmas is the identification of a particular religion with all religions. For example, the criticisms levelled against the religion and religionists of our contemporary society, quoted above, do not *necessarily* represent attacks on religion as such. It would be more accurate – and more objective – to view them as criticisms of the beliefs and behaviour of Christian Churches, and the general misuse of religion. Earlier we examined briefly the opposition of the Church to scientific discoveries and breakthroughs over several centuries. It would be irrational, however, to conclude that religion in general, or Christianity in particular, are by nature in direct conflict with science, or that religions necessarily retard human progress. Examined more critically, it can be seen that the Christian Church of the Middle Ages opposed the progress of science, not because it is in the general nature of religion to do so, but rather because the Church at that time represented a religion which had become corrupted for many reasons, among them being the incorporation of Greek philosophical ideas, the literal interpretation of the Bible and the pursuit of power and self glorification by those who played the role of its leaders. It was the Christian Church of medieval Europe, a religious institution in decline, which should be seen as the true source of the religious opposition to reason and science. There are also those who point out that from the very beginning the authority of the Church was self-appointed and hence its subsequent actions cannot be representative of Christianity, let alone other religions.[5]

What could there be in Christianity itself that might set it against scientific progress? Throughout the centuries, the stubborn adherence to very literal interpretations of the Bible by the mainstream Churches and many fundamentalist offshoots has undoubtedly provided the major source of conflict between science and religion, and continues to do so in the present day. However, an examination of some of the teachings of the New Testament reveals a different approach. For example, 'God . . . hath made us able ministers of the New Testament; not of the letter, but of the spirit; for the letter killeth, but the spirit giveth life',[6] seems to suggest that such literal interpretations of the Bible are specifically discouraged. Nevertheless, it is this clinging to the literal 'letter' that has contributed so significantly to the growing schism between science and religion and added fuel to the age-long dispute. It has also tended to polarise public opinion to a marked degree, and alienated many potential supporters, despite the fact that many leading theologians within the ecclesiastical hierarchy have drawn attention to the symbolic nature of Biblical historical accounts and parables.

The great mistake of the contemporary critical attitude to religion is to generalise from this picture of the Christian Church to Christianity itself, and then to religion and all other religions, viewing them as outdated, illogical and, even worse, irrelevant. This viewpoint is reached without any systematic investigation of the non-Christian religions which are nevertheless drawn into the conclusion. We have already discussed the tremendous impact of Islam on scientific progress, and the point may perhaps be clear that to model Christianity and all other religions on the Christian Church of the Middle Ages, and to tar them all with the same brush, is clearly not objective.

There are, in addition, two other very common dogmas or misconceptions regarding religion which are mentioned briefly here. A more detailed discussion of them will be found in the next chapter. One is to apply the reductionist method to all phenomena in a materialistic way and to confuse it with the scientific method (already described). Reductionism is used to reduce all phenomena to material causes and naturally filters out divine and spiritual phenomena. An example of the application of this method can be seen in the rejection of the possibility of a Creator and a Design for the Universe, or the existence of a divine purpose for man. Such issues are normally dismissed as unimportant, since they cannot be tested or proved. It could be argued, however, that this philosophy is against the true spirit of scientific method, since one cannot deduce that spiritual or divine phenomena do not exist simply because one cannot directly measure or observe them. As we shall see, there are a number of fundamental scientific assumptions which are also untestable, but which nevertheless remain central to scientific investigation.

The other common dogma is to deny or overlook the possibility of the existence of fundamental limits to man's comprehension. Essential to this dogma is the belief that science will in time explain and determine all phenomena. However, to presume that science does not have limits is in itself irrational; there is no evidence to support such a view.

The Bahá'í Faith and the science-religion conflict

The Bahá'í Faith is presented here, since it is the only world religion to date which explicitly discusses the relationship between science and religion.

The Bahá'í Faith arose in Persia in the mid-nineteenth century, at precisely that point in history when the greatest battles between the Christian Church and the protagonists of the scientific establishment were being fought. One of the important principles of this religion is that religious truth is relative, like scientific truth. This represents a marked departure from the claims to absolute truth made by certain followers of previous religions. A corollary of this is the acceptance of all the great teachers, including Abraham, Moses, Christ, Muhammad and Buddha. It explains that religious truth is in part relative to the time and place in which it is revealed, and that this is the reason for a continual succession of religions through history. Each religion brings a greater measure of understanding to the world, contributing to the never-ending spiritual and social development of the human race. Each religion is seen as consisting of two parts. One part deals with moral and spiritual values, with the exposition of divine truths and essential principles, which are repeated unchanged in all the great religions of the world. The second part consists of teachings and laws concerned with the practical and social requirements of the time. This part changes according to the evolution of human society and its changing needs, and consequently varies from religion to religion.

Another important teaching in the Bahá'í Faith which concerns us here is the independent investigation of truth. Bahá'ís are counselled to examine the specific claims and study the teachings of other religions at their authentic source. It is not sufficient to accept

second-hand accounts, since these may greatly misrepresent the
original teachings. They are also counselled to have great humility in
their own faith, and to respect the faith of others.[7] This search for
religious truth calls for the application of reason and judgement.
'Abdu'l-Bahá (1844–1921), the son of the founder of the Bahá'í
Faith, stated:

> Consider what it is that singles man out from among created
> beings, and makes of him a creature apart. Is it not his reasoning
> power, his intelligence? Shall he not make use of these in his
> study of religion? I say unto you: weigh carefully in the balance of
> reason and science everything that is presented to you as religion.
> If it passes this test, then accept it, for it is truth! If however, it
> does not so conform, then reject it, for it is ignorance![8]

It is in the balance of reason and science that religious ideas are to be
weighed, for scientific methods are part of the gift by which we will
learn to understand God's creation. Science is itself elevated to the
spiritual level.[9] It therefore follows that our scientific knowledge,
which is derived from the application of this God-given gift, cannot
be in conflict with true and uncorrupted religion, since this is also
revealed to humanity through the operation of the same divine will.

On the damaging effects of the misrepresentation of religion by
religious leaders and the benefits to humanity if science and religion
were to be in harmony, 'Abdu'l-Bahá said the following:

> Many religious leaders have grown to think that the importance
> of religion lies mainly in the adherence to a collection of certain
> dogmas and the practice of rites and ceremonies! Those whose
> souls they profess to cure are taught to believe likewise, and these
> cling tenaciously to the outward forms, confusing them with the
> inward truth.
>
> Now, these forms and rituals differ in the various churches and
> amongst the different sects, and even contradict one another;
> giving rise to discord, hatred, and disunion. The outcome of all
> this dissension is the belief of many cultured men that religion
> and science are contradictory terms, that religion needs no powers
> of reflection, and should in no wise be regulated by science, but
> must of necessity be opposed, the one to the other. The

unfortunate effect of this is that science has drifted apart from religion, and religion has become a mere blind and more or less apathetic following of the precepts of certain religious teachers, who insist on their own favourite dogmas being accepted even when they are contrary to science. This is foolishness, for it is quite evident that science is the light, and, being so, religion truly so-called does not oppose knowledge . . . Much of the discord and disunion of the world is created by these man-made oppositions and contradictions. If religion were in harmony with science and they walked together, much of the hatred and bitterness now bringing misery to the human race would be at an end. [10]

He went so far as to say: 'If religion is the cause of discord, then it is better to do without it'[11] – but he stated that this would not be necessary:

When religion, shorn of its superstitions, traditions and unintelligent dogmas shows its conformity with science, then there will be a great unifying, cleansing force in the world which will sweep before it all wars, disagreements, discords and struggles, and then will mankind be united in the power of the love of God.[12]

Elsewhere 'Abdu'l-Bahá states that this corruption of the original teachings of the religious founders is not confined to Christianity but is equally applicable to other world religions:

All religions of the present day have fallen into superstitious practices, out of harmony alike with the true principles of the teaching they represent and with the scientific discoveries of the time.[13]

It is fair to ask, of course, exactly how reason and science are to be applied to the investigation and understanding of religious matters. Science has its special methods for testing its insights. So long as they give a convincing account of observable data and cannot be proved wrong by evidence to the contrary, scientific theories stand up. By disproving religious dogmas which give a false account of material reality, such as the religious belief that Ptolemy's astronomy must be correct, this scientific approach makes a contribution to the sifting of essential religious truth from man-made religious fallacy. But how are the irreducible religious beliefs to be tested – belief in the existence of God, or the wholly unempirical beliefs that divided the early Christians: is Christ a creation of God or is he himself divine? There are perhaps two principles which can help us when dealing with such issues.

The first of these is the admonition to investigate the truth *independently*. Religious faith in the West has become synonymous with blind belief. However, while religious truth must ulitmately be taken on faith, this faith need not be blind. Although there are many religious beliefs that cannot be tested in the traditional manner in which scientific hypotheses related to the material world are tested and observed, yet it should not be assumed that we are therefore obliged to abandon our rational faculty when dealing with such issues. Indeed a whole-hearted acceptance of religious beliefs is unlikely unless both heart and mind are satisfied. The Bahá'í Faith stresses that one must examine religion with a spirit of independent investigation of truth, leaving behind one's prejudices and pre-conceptions. Weighing religious doctrines and tenets "in the balance of reason and science" can enable us to distinguish the pure or essential elements of a religion from erroneous traditions and man-made dogmas.

Bahá'u'lláh (1817–1892), the founder of the Bahá'í Faith, quoting a famous Sufi poet, referred to "the science of the love of God",[14] while Shoghi Effendi, his great-grandson, writes that the Bahá'í Faith is "scientific in its method'.[15] These are significant statements as they indicate very clearly that a major point of unity between science and religion is not so much related to the objects of their inquiry but lies rather in their scientific method of investiga-tion, an approach which should be applied to both scientific and religious quests. Above all, the proper application of reason to religious beliefs enables one to obtain a far deeper understanding than is possible to achieve with an attitude of obedient and unquestioning faith. The new religious insights we can thus acquire in turn reinforce our faith. Only an insecure religion would actively discourage its followers from applying their God-given gift of reason to matters of religion while at the same time upholding the belief that God, in whose image we are made, is a conscious and reasonable being.

The second principle which can assist us in the application of reason to religion is to ask what the *fruits* of a given religion or religious belief may be. We must, however, make a careful distinction between the behaviour of the professed adherents to a religion and the religion itself. While it is true that the fruits of a religious belief *should* be recognisable in the actions of a believer, the conduct of the followers should never be the *sole* criterion for assessing a religion. There are other criteria, such as the life of the founder and the quality of his teachings, which one can investigate and assess. For example, do the Ten Commandments of the Old Testament represent constructive and valuable social principles, especially in the socio-historical context in which they were given? Do the teachings, 'Love thy neighbour as thyself' in Christianity and 'No one of you is a believer until he desires for his brother that which he desires for himself' in Islam, which are variously found in other religions, constitute important social and moral ideals towards which the believers are urged to strive?

All the major religions known to man stress spiritual principles such as the importance of love, truthfulness, concern for others etc. Such principles are not empirically testable in any scientific sense. However, it may be argued that if belief in an unempirical notion puts mankind on the path to social progress and unity, or assists us to better understand ourselves or the world, it must be right to so believe. Empirically untestable generalities are in any event indispensable to any system of belief, and religion cannot be faulted for having them. Science itself uses them. Faith in the existence of universal laws which can be tested is a precondition of scientific investigation. This faith is ultimately subjective, and no amount of scientific analysis can give indisputable proof for its use. Rather the success of scientific investigation, or its fruits as it were, stand as the only indicators by which its validity can be assessed, and thus it falls into the same category as the great untestable truths of religion.

This chapter has traced the development of a principle that has much in common with religious belief: our faith in the reliability of the material world to behave with enough regularity to make a scientific method possible. This is surely one of those empirically untestable beliefs that has brought humankind closer to unity, through a nearly universal respect for and participation in the scientific enterprise. It has resulted in the alleviation of many forms of human suffering, and has helped us to progress in the development of our natural gifts.

There is another untestable generality, however, that is often identified with the scientific revolution as well. Many would count it a scientific truth, that all that exists is material and that everything that happens is determined by mechanical changes in material things. This is the thesis of materialistic determinism. It arises by subtracting a relatively peripheral God from the vast mechanisms constructed as models of the universe by Descartes and Newton. If it is a truth, scientific or otherwise, then science has surely supplanted religion as the only way to understand reality. Chapter 2 will be concerned with considering this possibility, arguing in general against materialism, and in particular against its use in evolutionary theory.

2. HUMAN EVOLUTION
By Accident or Design?

In only a few decades of our unique period in human history, we have experienced a rapid and vast process of change. We are now beset with unprecedented challenges and staggering responsibilities. Scientific developments have made possible a revolution in technology and communications, and humanity has as a consequence reached a condition of unavoidable social, economic and political interdependence. The immediate repercussions almost everywhere of even very distant events mean that old boundaries, whether natural or political, are becoming less and less meaningful. The planet can no longer be divided into non-interacting regions, and the pressing problems are all of them global ones.

The scientific revolution that made all of this possible has at the same time done little to teach us the art of living in a global community. Our future is perilously unpredictable. The lessons learnt from the past seem desperately inadequate as guides to our own age; yet if unspeakable horrors are to be averted, immediate action must be taken. Terrorism and violence have become an international norm as Third World poverty and North–South inequality confront the political paralysis of our world system. A menace of global proportions jeopardises the very survival of the human race as our planet faces overpopulation, devastation of the natural environment and an East–West arms race that threatens to end in nuclear conflagration.

It is tempting to say that, if these are the fruits of scientific development, then we must after all have been set on the wrong course four hundred years ago by men like Galileo. However, placing faith in scientific method is surely not a mistake. The fault lies in making this faith exclusive and all-embracing – in expecting the scientific outlook to give us every conceivable form of wisdom that we can need. This is what happens when we allow ourselves to think that materialism is an essential part of the scientific outlook – when we begin to say that it is unscientific to acknowledge the existence of anything apart from material objects or to explain events in terms of anything more than mechanical changes in matter.

In biology, the ascendancy of this deterministic view since the middle of the nineteenth century has convinced us that human evolution must be blind, that our development, both biological and cultural, is an outcome of chance. It has made us look backward for an understanding of our true nature – to some accidental event that is supposed to have fixed our behavioural tendencies within the chemistry of our genes – rather than forward to an unravelling divine truth. We have been led to believe that we are irredeemably aggressive and warlike. What is worse, we have been presented in evolutionary theory with a mechanism called 'the survival of the fittest' which has been readily absorbed as a model for our own behaviour. As the world approaches the point at which all, fit and unfit, must perish together unless we act together, surely the time has come to reassess this materialist, survivalist philosophy.

Materialistic Theories of Evolution

The medieval picture of nature retreated only by stages. It became commonplace to conceive of the earth as just one of a system of planets revolving round the sun, and it was decided that Scripture did not really conflict with this view; only Greek science was discredited by the new astronomy. A literal reading continued to be given to the biblical story of creation by almost everyone up until the mid-nineteenth century. Then the Christian world was deeply shaken by a growing conviction among naturalists that the geology of the earth and the life upon it had evolved over billions of years. The scientific frame of mind that wanted to recognise the fact of evolution had to confront a religious frame of mind that refused to. In this polarised climate, scientists tended to uproot themselves from the religious past altogether, in a way that Galileo and Newton had not, seeking a purely materialist account of life on earth.

Evolutionary theory before Darwin

Evolution was not a particularly new idea in the nineteenth century. Ancient Greek biologists had noted the existence of vestigial organs such as the human appendix and suggested that these were evidence that organisms had developed through time, adapting to changing circumstances. (This was another idea of Aristotle's that St Thomas Aquinas did not make into official Catholic doctrine.) The notion received fresh attention when doubts began to arise about the ability of geology to reconcile its findings with Bible-inspired calculations of the age of the earth.

The Irish Archbishop James Ussher (1581–1656) had added up the ages of Old Testament patriarchs and fixed the year of the Creation as 4004 BC. Later, Dr Lightfoot, Vice-Chancellor of the University of Cambridge, made a careful study of the Book of Genesis and gave greater precision to the date: 9.00 a.m. on 23 October of the same year. However, according to the eleventh edition of the *Encyclopaedia Britannica,* this date was one hundred and fifty-three years out! The new spirit of observation, including a taste for collecting fossils, began to put a strain on this 6,000-year time-scale, and reputable geologists of the late seventeenth century felt a need for theories that could reconcile Scripture with what they saw. Among their published works are accounts of the whole of the world's fossil-bearing strata being laid down in a few months following the Great Flood. In 1696 Whiston published his book, *A New Theory of the Earth wherein the Creation of the World in Six Days, the Universal Deluge, and the General Conflagration, as laid down in the Holy Scriptures, are shown to be perfectly agreeable to Reason and Philosophy.* Here it was explained how a comet might have caused the Flood, and how the ensuing upheavals might have shaped the earth's surface as we know it today.

In 1788, however, the Scottish geologist James Hutton (1726–97) published his *Theory of the Earth,* the first such work to be inspired by the new science. He proposed that past changes in the earth's surface were due to causes that are still in operation now. The same processes slowly altering coastlines today, or changing the

elevations of mountain peaks, were also responsible for the disappear-
ance of continents and depositions of great rock sediments in the
past. This 'uniformitarian' account gave little credence to the sudden
catastrophes of one sort or another that were supposed to have
brought about the great events etched in the geological record.
These events, thought Hutton and his supporters, must have
occurred slowly over a period of billions of years.

Another strain on the literal interpretation of Scripture was
zoology's burgeoning collection of newly discovered species. It was
the official view of most Christian churches and sects that all animals
now existing were descended from individuals carried by Noah in
the Ark. Any species not saved by him had become extinct. But it
now began to emerge how vast the Ark would have needed to be if a
male and a female of each of the millions of different species now
living had been on board. There was also a question about the
distribution of species. Australia and the Americas are a long way
from Mount Ararat in the eastern part of present-day Turkey, where
the Ark is said to have discharged its cargo after the Flood. How
could the distinctive species of these continents have travelled so far
and left not even a trace of their kind along the way?

Evolutionary ideas were popular in early nineteenth-century
France, where a strongly anticlerical tradition had taken root after
the clergy sided with the aristocracy during the Revolution of
1798–9. Jean Baptiste Lamarck (1744–1829) gave a thoroughly
materialist explanation of evolution in which modifications induced
in an individual by its changing environment are transmitted to
offspring. The Comte de Saint-Simon (1760–1825) and Auguste
Comte (1798–1857) were developing at the same time a materialist
view of man and society in their philosophy of 'positivism', which
denied the possibility of any but scientific knowledge. Comte
claimed to have founded a science of social change and development
and he attempted to propagate positivism as a new religion. In
several countries positivist societies were formed to worship
humanity in place of God.

Many nineteenth-century British thinkers were influenced by
French positivism. One of these was Herbert Spencer (1820–1903),
who propounded a theory of evolution which he said was both
philosophical and scientific. It proposed that all change within any

structure is in the direction of increasing differentiation and heterogeneity and at the same time in the direction of increasing integration and coherence. This view is philosophical, he said, because it claims to be true of everything, but it is also scientific, because it is confirmed by observation, both of the natural world and of the development of human society.

Darwin

The name that for millions has come to be synonymous with evolutionary theory is that of Charles Darwin (1809–82). Although his grandfather Erasmus Darwin had been an evolutionist, publishing a theory similar to Lamarck's in the 1790s, Charles Darwin as a young man believed in the strict and literal truth of the Bible, and his family had intentions of his becoming a clergyman. As an undergraduate at Cambridge, however, he began a gradual progression away from these beliefs. Among his personal friends at Cambridge was Charles Lyell (1797–1875), whose text *The Principles of Geology* (1830–3) expounded Hutton's uniformitarianism. In 1831, at the age of twenty-two, Darwin was taken on as a naturalist by Captain Robert Fitzroy of the British naval survey ship HMS *Beagle*, and he spent the years 1832–6 studying at first hand the geography, geology and wildlife of South America. Fossils of sea life found in the high Andes helped to persuade Darwin of the long age of the earth. He observed slight differences between populations of the same species of birds and tortoises isolated from one another on different islands of the Galapagos group, and this indicated to him that species change over time. Long hours of argument with a Bible-literal Fitzroy helped to crystallise these views.

Back in England in 1838, Darwin read a book by Thomas Malthus (1766–1834). First published in 1798, this *Essay on the Principle of Populations* commented on the consequences of 'superfecundity', the production of more young by human populations than are required to replace their parents. Darwin applied this concept to plants and animals and drew a conclusion of his own which he believed explained the mechanism by which evolution occurs: populations produce more individuals than can survive on the resources available, and so there is a struggle between individuals for these resources, with only the fittest of them surviving. Darwin thought that even the slightest heritable variations between individual members of a population would tend to be reflected in the outcome of the struggle; individuals with even a slight advantage over others would tend to survive and reproduce. If parts of a population became isolated in different environments, as species in the Galapagos had been, the slight variance of environmental pressures would select for distinct races of these species. Over extremely long periods, distinct species would emerge; populations gradually adapted to very different environmental niches. Darwin gave the names 'natural selection' and 'survival of the fittest' to this process. He believed that by long and very gradual natural selection, all of the millions of species on earth developed from previously existing species, and that at the stem of a very complex family tree there is probably one simple form of life. He believed that humans and apes are descended from a common but now extinct primate ancestor.

Conscious of the distress he would cause to religious believers if he published this view, Darwin for many years shared his thoughts only with close friends. However, a Welsh naturalist, Alfred Russel Wallace (1823–1913), a professional specimen collector who had travelled in South America and the Malay archipelago, had also read the essay on populations by Malthus and had also conceived the idea of a mechanism of survival of the fittest. Impressed by Darwin's published journal of the voyage of the *Beagle,* Wallace sent a draft of the survivalist thesis to a thunderstruck Darwin for comment. Darwin was forced to publish his idea if he was to have any credit for its originality. His *Origin of Species* appeared in 1859.

The development of Darwinism

Scientific controversy over Darwin's mechanism began with his inadequate account of how variation arises and is maintained. He speculated that the cells of an organism produce minute particles, which he called 'gemmules', that circulate freely in the organism and are transmitted to offspring. Taking a leaf from the book of his grandfather and from Lamarck, he said that gemmules became changed when the organism acquires new characteristics. For example, if a normally tall plant is dwarfed in unfavourable conditions, this will affect the gemmules, and there will be a tendency for offspring to be dwarfed as well. Darwin also stated that there is a 'blending' of the parents' gemmules in the offspring. The influence of each parent on the inheritance is roughly half; the influence of each grandparent is roughly one quarter, and so on. Critics wondered why new variations were not simply diluted out, and Darwin's reply would seem to be that the Lamarckian mechanism and natural selection work together. Change in the environment, caused for example by a population's becoming established on a new island, repeatedly affects the gemmules of members of the population; and the environment also selects for survival those members of the population inheriting a sufficient blend of these useful gemmules.

Francis Galton (1822–1911), a cousin of Darwin, attempted and failed to find experimental evidence for these views by intertransfusing the blood of different colours of rabbits and recording the colours of the offspring. Neither blending nor any inheritance of environmentally induced variations could be found. This was one of the first steps towards the scientific rejection of Lamarckism. The notion of gemmules was discarded when in about 1900 the work of the Austrian monk Gregor Mendel (1822–84) came to light. Mendel had conducted experiments in cross-breeding peas that had led him to postulate the existence of physical factors that are inherited whole from one generation to the next, not blended. These were eventually to be called genes, and Mendel's work was to be refined as the theory of recessive and dominant traits in inheritance.

Genes solved a problem for Darwinism, because now there was no puzzle about what kept a new variation from being diluted out of a population. It need be introduced only once, and so long as it continued to be selected for, it would spread unblended through succeeding generations of the original variant's descendants. A new problem arose, however, because botanists became convinced by experimental findings that gradual changes were insufficient to explain evolution. They believed that evolution occurred in abrupt spurts when large-scale changes in the genes of an organism (mutations) took place and the organism passed the mutated genes on to offspring. According to this view, changes were not gradually selected – they emerged suddenly. On the other hand, palaeonto-

logists examining the fossil record at this time did not believe in
evolutionary jumps, and continued to support Darwinian gradualism.

Developments in the 1920s and 1930s led to the rise of modern
population genetics, which stresses the harmful nature of most
mutations. Only small-scale mutations were thought to improve
adaptability, and Darwin's gradualist view, operated by natural
selection, came back into favour. A newly emerging combination of
Darwinism and the views of geneticists was described by Julian
Huxley in his book *The Modern Synthesis* in 1942. According to
this synthesis, small and entirely random genetic mutations con-
tinually occur, creating variations between individuals. Natural
selection determines mechanically which of these variations will
survive.

The new synthesis was reinforced in the 1940s by the discovery of
the complex nucleic acid DNA and its role in carrying genetic
information. In the decades since, molecular biology has been able to
construct a model in which the genes are segments of chromosomes
composed of DNA, the related nucleic acid RNA and associated
proteins. The original fertilised single cell destined to grow into an
offspring receives a set of chromosomes from each parent; one set is
already part of the structure of the unfertilised egg cell, and the
other is introduced into the cell by the sperm. Pairs of matching
chromosomes, one from each parent, intertwine to form double-
stranded structures. As the original cell multiplies, each chromosome pair is duplicated, and finally the new organism has an
identical set of them tightly bundled in the nucleus of each of its
cells, which may number thousands of millions.

The chemistry of the chromosomes is like a set of computer
programs. A program makes a computer behave one way rather than
another by controlling the opening and closing of electrical switches
in the computer's circuitry in response to inputs. Similarly,
chromosomes control the kind of protein that the cell containing
them will manufacture in response to stimuli. As the organism
grows, chemical stimuli from other cells switch off most of a new
cell's chromosomal programs but leave some running – not the same
ones in every cell. This enables the cells to specialise, some obeying
the program that makes a cell into hair, others obeying the program
that makes a cell into muscle tissue, and so on.

A gene is a chromosome segment controlling the manufacture of proteins affecting a specific feature, such as hair colour or hair texture. The matching genes in a chromosome pair may conflict in what they tell the cell to do. The gene for hair colour inherited from the mother may have a chemical structure that would cause the cell to make proteins that produce a black pigment, while the gene inherited from the father may have a chemical structure that would cause so little pigment to be produced that blond hair would result. In such conflicts, one gene tends to be dominant, chemically switching off the operation of the other, which is called recessive. Dominant genes are more likely to show up in the visible traits of a population, but a recessive gene will sometimes function, as when both parents carry it and both pass it on to one of their offspring, whose cells then contain only the recessive gene.

A genetic mutation is a change in the chemical structure of the DNA molecule in a chromosome. This is considered by the modern synthesis to be always an accidental disruption, caused, for example, by random penetrations of the cell by background radiation. The chemical change may give rise to a variation in the manufacture of proteins in the cell affected; the cell is reprogrammed. If the DNA of an egg cell or a sperm cell is reprogrammed in this way, the change is heritable – it may be duplicated in every cell of a new organism, which could in turn pass the new program on to further generations. According to the modern synthesis, most mutations are harmful and survive in the population, if at all, only as recessive genes, so that only offspring inheriting the mutation from both parents will suffer. A tiny number of mutations, however, are said accidentally to create an advantage in a given environment, and these will contribute to the evolutionary progression.

Although the genetic part of this synthesis has been very successful, controversy has arisen once again over the pace of evolution. In the 1940s misgivings about the gradualism of the orthodox model arose among a small number of researchers examining the fossil record.[1] In the early 1970s these doubts began to emerge more seriously,[2] and there is today a debate between gradualists and punctuationists, the latter detecting in the fossil record large, rapid changes in species, separated by long periods of very little change. It has been suggested that this phenomenon may be reconciled with the modern synthesis if it can be argued that sudden appearances of rapid changes are due to the isolation of small, inbred sub-populations in conditions of quickening environmental change.

Modern biology

Whatever the adjustments that evolutionary theory may make as the history of the life sciences unfolds, most biologists seem to be confident that it will forever conform to four underlying assumptions:

1 that chance is the basic mechanism of the universe;
2 that the necessity of a certain trait for survival is all that can explain why organisms have that trait;
3 that humans are simply animals and all of their unique qualities, such as language, intellect and the distinctively human emotions, have appeared in us by chance and been preserved solely because of their survival value;
4 that all mental and biological phenomena can be reduced to biochemical reactions obeying the laws of physics – all psychological phenomena are to be explained in terms of biological ones, which are to be explained in turn by chemical ones, and those by physics.

The French molecular biologist Jacques Monod, winner of the Nobel Prize for physiology and medicine in 1965, goes so far as to say that assumption (1) is the only hypothesis 'compatible with observed and tested fact'. He stresses that assumption (1) is prior to assumption (2):

We say that [mutations] are accidental, due to chance. And since they constitute the only possible source of modifications in the genetic text, itself the sole repository of the organism's hereditary structures, it necessarily follows that chance alone is the source of every innovation, of all creation in the biosphere. Pure chance, absolutely free but blind, at the very root of the stupendous edifice of evolution: this central concept of modern biology is no longer one among other possible or even conceivable hypotheses. It is today the sole conceivable hypothesis, the only one compatible with observed and tested fact. And nothing warrants the supposition (or the hope) that conceptions about this should, or ever could, be revised.[3]

Monod derives from them assumptions (3) and (4):

the linguistic capacity revealed in the course of the brain's epigenetic development is today part of 'human nature', itself defined with the genome in the radically different language of the genetic code. A miracle? Certainly, since in the final analysis language too was a product of chance.[4]

Assumption (4) had already been voiced by Darwin's friend and early supporter, Thomas Huxley:

Zoological physiology is the doctrine of the functions or actions of animals. It regards animal bodies as machines impelled by various forces and performing a certain amount of work which can be expressed in terms of the ordinary forces of nature. The final object of physiology is to deduce the facts of morphology, on the one hand, and those of ecology on the other, from the laws of molecular forces of matter.[5]

The sentiment is echoed more forcefully today by Richard Dawkins:

We are survival machines – robot vehicles blindly programmed to preserve the selfish molecules known to us as genes.[6]

Konrad Lorenz assigns the complete history of human knowledge to material causes:

I shall . . . consider human understanding in the same way as any other phylogenetically evolved function which serves the purpose of survival, that is, as a function of a natural physical system interacting with a physical external world.[7]

Criticisms of the Materialist View

Mention that you disagree with Darwin and you may easily be taken for a creationist, one of those defenders of fundamentalist religion who are determined to use any argument they can find in order to retain a literal reading of the Bible's story of creation. In many minds – both exclusively scientific and exclusively religious ones – this is what an objection to orthodox evolutionary theory is bound to amount to. If this were true, I believe I would prefer to be a Darwinian, for the creationist view is incapable of adopting a spirit of scientific inquiry. It selects data in a prejudiced way as though for a legal proceeding. Since the creationists consider it an obligation of faith to accept the Bible word for word, vast collections of geological and fossil data indicating a long history of the earth, with changing forms of life, are discounted on grounds that seem forced and contrived.

By its anti-scientific stance and concentration on the bare issue of whether evolution has occurred, creationism does great harm to religion. A picture of the religious frame of mind as hopelessly unscientific has become imprinted on the minds of many scientists. By equating Darwinism with the notion of evolution itself, creationists have also obscured the central issue raised by *The Origin of Species*. Evolution was an old idea with a following among many naturalists long before Darwin. These naturalists were prepared to accept it as a piece of data to be explained, and so am I. But Darwin and those contributing to the development of this theory go beyond the limits of science and venture into philosophical speculation when they imply that evolution is blind.

Objective knowledge

In order to assess the claims of Jacques Monod and other modern biologists it is first necessary to define objective knowledge, because so-called 'objectivity' is often invoked as the guiding principle of these claims. Objective knowledge can be defined as that knowledge which is derived from the use of the scientific method, and hence is synonymous with scientific knowledge. It will be recalled from the discussion on scientific method in Chapter 1 that, before one can replace an existing hypothesis, one must demonstrate its limitations and propose a new hypothesis which does not have the same limitations. One must then confirm the new hypothesis by experiment, and the experimental results must be repeatable. Thus science never proves theories; rather, it *dis*proves them. Objective or scientific knowledge is consequently a succession of ever-improving hypotheses. Knowledge is gained when an existing hypothesis is disproved. In Karl Popper's phrase, scientific progress is a series of 'conjectures and refutations'.[8]

An important point to bear in mind therefore is that scientific or objective knowledge is relative, not absolute, and is always subject to modification and improvement. In other words, there is no question of ever establishing an 'absolute proof' for the accuracy of a hypothesis. All that can be said is that a hypothesis explains the existing data better than any other model known at any given time. The objectivity of science therefore lies in its method rather than in the particular nature of the object or phenomenon that it investigates. There are many hypotheses which are untestable for one reason or another. It may be that a technological restriction exists on the currently available tools of experimentation, as is often the case. For example, at present it is impossible to decide with any degree of certainty whether the universe is finite or infinite. More data are required before the question can be adequately answered. This in turn requires better tools of experimentation and observation. The correct course of action under these circumstances is to avoid making a scientific comment and to delay the acceptance of such a hypothesis. If one does comment, then one is expressing a belief, not objective knowledge.

The limits of science

There are also phenomena which cannot be scientifically tested even in principle, like those of religion, ethics and metaphysics. They represent a fundamental limit to objective or scientific knowledge. The existence of God, for instance, is impossible to test even in principle; science proceeds on finite, definable hypotheses, but God by definition is infinite and undefinable. Clearly the finite cannot test the infinite. This is equally true for the hypothesis of an overall purpose to life and the universe. Since it is a hypothesis which proposes an infinitely complex design, it can never be completely validated *or disproved* by the finite methods of scientific experiment. One cannot, even in a thought experiment, conceive of a way of testing such a hypothesis; it would require an experiment that is infinitely complex and infinitely wide-ranging in space, time and possibility. If a scientific theory claims to refute the existence of a grand design in the universe or in life on earth, then it is manifestly subjective – a belief and not objective knowledge. In fact, it may be asserted that all the fundamental questions such as the existence of God, a purpose to the universe and the origin of life fall into the category of untestable hypotheses and hence lie outside the domain of objective knowledge.

However, the fact that science cannot test such hypotheses does not make them unimportant. If there is a design and purpose for the existence of the human species then it would be a great error indeed to discard it, whether in the name of objectivity or for any other reason. It is unavoidable that we should make suppositions about matters lying beyond the scope of science. What is to be avoided is the misapprehension that these suppositions are scientific, and the misapprehension that everything worth saying is scientific. As Karl Popper expresses it:

> science does not make assertions about ultimate questions – about the riddles of existence, or about man's task in the world. This has often been well understood. But some great scientists, and many lesser ones, have misunderstood the situation. The fact that science cannot make any pronouncement about ethical principles has been misinterpreted as indicating that there are no such principles, while in fact the search for truth presupposes ethics.[9]

In his book *The Limits of Science,* Peter Medawar makes a similar point:

> That there is indeed a limit upon science is made very likely by the existence of questions that science cannot answer and that no conceivable advance of science would empower it to answer. These are the questions that children ask – the 'ultimate questions' of Karl Popper. I have in mind such questions as: How did everything begin? What are we all here for? What is the point of living? Doctrinaire positivism – now something of a period piece – dismissed all such questions as nonquestions or pseudo-questions such as only simpletons ask and only charlatans of one kind or another profess to be able to answer. This peremptory dismissal leaves one empty and dissatisfied because the questions make sense to those who ask them, and the answers, to those who try to give them; but whatever else may be in dispute, it would be universally agreed that it is not to science that we should look for answers.[10]

There is another possible limit on science. Scientific knowledge is derived from the intellectual faculty of the human mind. Could not this faculty have intrinsic limitations? Just as the vegetable world cannot comprehend the animal world, or the animal world comprehend the human world, so too perhaps the human intellect may not be able to comprehend or confirm the existence of other worlds. Another way of illustrating this is to liken the human mind to a fishing net. A fishing net is restricted to catching fish larger than the dimensions of the mesh comprising it, and in the sea of life the human mind may also be restricted in what it can perceive and what it can comprehend. Indeed, to assume it is not runs contrary to experience: all forms of life are restricted and limited in some way. It is important at least to acknowledge that this possibility exists.

Some materialists say that it is intolerable to encourage in any way propositions which lie beyond the scope of science. If they lie beyond the scope of science then there is no way in principle that any observable data could show them to be true or false. They are irrefutable, fitting the data no matter what data may occur. Scientifically, they are therefore superfluous, giving us no direction in which to inquire, no particular data to deduce. If we ask what data we should find, they simply tell us that *whatever* data we find can be explained. Materialist philosophers have protested that, under these conditions, the propositions of ethics, religion and metaphysics cannot even be said to mean anything.

True enough, religious beliefs are not scientific hypotheses. However, neither is materialism a scientific hypothesis; it is a piece of philosophy, something that equally fits all the data, come what may. The insight that all is material and determined by chance can have no more experimental disproof than the insight that God exists and chooses the shape of the universe. There are millions upon millions of events in the universe for which material explanations have not been found; but these are not refutations of materialism, for that principle is no more than an expression of *faith* that science could, if it had infinite resources and infinite time, explain everything that there is in terms of a reduction to atoms and molecules. This materialism is not a *finding* of science, then. It is a presupposition of some philosophers and scientists.

Scientific reductions

Another way of understanding the process of scientific method is to consider scientific hypotheses as reductions. A hypothesis models what may be a highly complex phenomenon on a relative framework of conception, an approximation of the real phenomenon; hence the procedure is one of reduction. The scientific method then proceeds by a series of ever-improving reductions, each initially tested and validated by experiment, and then later disproved by experiment.

There can be good and bad reductions. A good reduction is one that can be supported by experimental evidence. The beneficial results of such a reduction are well known — it usually leads to greater understanding of a particular phenomenon. A good reduction may unite two different fields of study previously thought to be unrelated. Thus it can greatly simplify existing hypotheses and lead to the proposal of new ones. An example of a good reduction is the one made by James Clerk Maxwell when he reduced the magnetic force to the electric force and vice versa. By this reduction he established an underlying unity between the magnetic and electric forces and initiated the study of just one force: the electromagnetic. Maxwell thereby greatly enriched scientific understanding of these phenomena.

A bad reduction is one that cannot be substantiated by experimental evidence and is essentially misleading. It usually has the effect of obscuring good reductions and retarding the progress of scientific understanding. An example of a reduction which is not fully tested by experiment in physics is the search for a unified field theory to reduce the four forces of nature, the gravitational, electromagnetic, weak and strong forces, into one force. Although many physicists hope that a unified field theory will be confirmed by experiment, they are fully aware of the lack of experimental evidence to support it. Thus to claim that a unified theory is confirmed by science would at this moment constitute a bad reduction. A bad reduction is one that lies in the realm of speculation; it is merely a belief and should not be put forward as objective knowledge.

Bad reductions of the modern synthesis

The four major assumptions which are among the fundamental articles of faith of modern biologists, and to which we referred earlier, should now be assessed in the light of the above for their scientific objectivity. These are all assumptions which most biologists consider to provide definitive answers to some of man's 'ultimate questions'. Do they constitute good or bad reductions?

The first claim is that pure chance is the basic mechanism of the universe and that there is no grand design or purpose to life on earth. The refutation of such a claim is simple. A scientific theory, even in principle, cannot test whether there is or is not a purpose to life on earth or to the universe. Such a hypothesis lies outside the bounds of objective or scientific knowledge as already explained; no experiment can be conceived which can adequately test this class of hypothesis. Then why, one may ask, is such an obviously bad reduction made? Many biologists base such a claim on an irrational extrapolation of theories in modern biology. It is derived from the assertion that chance, in the form of random perturbations, is the only possible means of modifying genetic information. Modifications of this type are achieved, they claim, through mis-copies of DNA. However, this extrapolation is misleading. Firstly, it presupposes a perfect knowledge of the entire genetic text on the DNA and the mechanism by which this information is transcribed. Apart from the fact that such a perfect knowledge does not exist, scientists should on principle never claim to have perfect knowledge in anything, even though the claim is implicit as in this case. Secondly, there are a growing number of scientists who do not think that all the information for an organism's growth and development is contained genetically in DNA and hence also refute the claim of chance as the fundamental and only mechanism of life.[11]

The British astronomer Fred Hoyle has argued that the detectable frequency of random useful mutations is far too low to be the cause of the observable differences between species. He has also calculated how unlikely it is that the first primitive form of life on earth could have begun by way of a random shuffling of molecules to form a minimum requirement of 2,000 enzyme molecules simultaneously from their twenty component amino acids; the probability is one in ten to the power of 40,000. This is 'as ridiculous and improbable', Hoyle says, 'as the proposition that a tornado blowing through a junkyard may assemble a Boeing 747'. He is moved to ask:

How has the Darwinian theory of evolution by natural selection managed, for upwards of a century, to fasten itself like a superstition on so-called enlightened opinion? Why is the theory still defended so vigorously? Personally, I have little doubt that scientific historians of the future will find it mysterious that a theory which could be seen to be unworkable came to be so widely believed. The explanation they offer will I think be based less on the erroneous nature of the theory itself and more on the social changes and historical circumstances that surround its development.[12]

In reply to Hoyle, it has been argued that the original life form could have been simpler than the one he envisages, and that the event of its spontaneous appearance had 100 million years of chances in which to appear. In fact, the arguments about what is probable and what is improbable remain inconclusive, because the materialists construct an event whose probability cannot be calculated — the structure of the original form of life that they postulate is unknown. This, of course, is somewhat different from saying that chance-and-necessity is the only hypothesis compatible with the evidence.

Neither the rejection of a grand design or purpose, nor the assertion that chance is the primary cause of all activity in the universe can be supported by scientific knowledge, even in principle. The latter, as we have seen, is an untestable hypothesis and lies outside the bounds of objective knowledge. Those who make such claims are expressing a belief, and their claims should not be considered to be objective or scientific. Unfortunately this misconception is freely transmitted to the public at large. Jacques Monod's book *Chance and Necessity*, which was specifically written to transmit concepts of modern biology to the public, goes as far as defining objectivity as meaning the lack of purpose and design. This stands in direct contradiction to the process of the scientific method, the foundation of all objective knowledge. Monod states:

The cornerstone of the scientific method is the postulate that nature is objective. In other words, the systematic denial that 'true' knowledge can be reached by interpreting phenomena in terms of final causes — that is to say 'purpose'.[13]

This quotation illustrates a common misconception that is not only found in modern biology. It involves a serious misuse of the term 'objectivity' and violates the principle of true objectivity so intricately associated with the correct use of scientific method.

An analogy can best illustrate the fallacy of concluding from current biological theory that there is no universal design. Imagine an infinitely complex computer whose circuitry is hidden from human sight except through a small number of 'portholes'. On looking through these holes one may observe a limited number of semiconductor switches operating in certain sequences. If measurements of electrical signals on these switches were made, one would detect two signals. Firstly, one would detect some computer-operating signals which represent the running of the computer; but since only a small part of the computer's circuitry can be observed, these signals would be mysterious, and their purpose could not be completely known. Secondly, one would detect the presence of random electrical fluctuations, known as electrical noise. If one were to conclude that the whole computer did not have any purpose, purely from the detection of random fluctuations (electrical noise), one would be in great error. Yet this deduction or reduction bears similarities to the claim that the perturbations that exist in the copying of DNA are by all appearances random, and that therefore life has no purpose. It is equivalent to saying that the computer-operating signals in the analogy are generated and entirely accounted for by the presence of electrical noise. Experience shows, however, that electrical noise or any other such random effect always averages out and does not produce large signals of its own accord. The question of purpose can obviously not be settled by gaining partial glimpses of the computer's circuitry, particularly if that circuitry is infinite in complexity, making it impossible to gain complete knowledge of its operation even in principle.

Another fallacy or bad reduction central to modern biology is that human beings are nothing but animals. This assumption has damaging effects beyond the confines of biological science. There is no evidence to suggest that man is only an animal, no evidence to suggest that the human mind is a simple extension of the central nervous system of an animal. Until detailed experimental evidence can be produced to show how the human mind has been derived from an animal brain, there may be no justification for such a statement. On the contrary, the special qualities of the human mind, such as free will, imagination etc., suggest that its characteristics may be fundamentally different from an animal's, as different as an animal's characteristics are from those of a plant. Not to consider this possibility is in itself subjective. We each experience our own choices as acts of free will and cannot escape viewing others, if we are to view them as human beings at all, as similarly making choices and exercising freedom. Yet the chance-and-necessity hypothesis is forced to deny that this is any more than an illusion. If human behaviour is the product of the same account of chance and necessity that the modern synthesis gives for animal behaviour, then it must be determined behaviour – not free, but resulting from a causal process in which the programs in our genes determine how we will respond to an input of stimuli from our environment. The chance-and-necessity thesis cannot avoid this kind of reductionism, but can this reductionism be said to be in any way satisfactory, let alone the only hypothesis compatible with observed and tested fact? The profound failure of materialists in psychology and the social sciences to develop reliable systems for predicting individual behaviour and social events must be considered a sign of weakness in the reductionist view. Consequently, the only safe conclusion based on current biological experimental evidence is merely that evolution has occurred. To stipulate at this moment exactly how would be a bad reduction. There is very little evidence on the transition state of 'ape to man', and such a reduction at present is extremely misleading.

A different aspect of this reduction may be illustrated with the help of another computer analogy. It has been concluded that, because we share some of the same proteins and other building blocks as other forms of life, human beings are therefore fundamentally no different from these forms of life. This is similar to saying that, because a computer and a simple transistor radio share some common components, such as diodes, they are essentially the same and one can be derived from the other. This again is clearly a great error; it does not take into account the possibility of the existence of software which drives the switches (hardware) of the computer. An infinite number of programs may exist which thus give it a very different character and purpose from the transistor radio.

One could only gain an understanding of this purpose if one were able to see the computer software or computer code of the system. In this analogy, questions that pertain to the computer's software correspond to questions dealt with by religion in the human world, and the questions that pertain to the hardware operation of the computer correspond to questions posed in the material world. The two aspects are complementary. Just as the hardware and software elements need to work in balance and harmony for the computer to function correctly, so too science and religion have complementary roles for the correct operation of human society and the individual. The software and hardware may also be looked upon as a way of representing the mind and matter of man. The history of humanity so far may be viewed as a struggle to harmonise both of these elements in human society and to give them their proper expression. The software instructions in a computer direct the activity of the hardware and give it purpose. Neither can exist without the other; an understanding of both disciplines is required for the normal running of the computer. Likewise, true religion spiritually directs the material affairs of humanity, giving them purpose and meaning. It is this sense of transcendental purpose which most clearly distinguishes human existence from that of an animal.

In assessing the claim that natural selection is the sole cause of development in every form of life on earth, one cannot help being struck by certain gaps in the evidence. For example, Darwinism implies that a gradual transition took place between reptiles and birds, and between wingless and winged insects. It is not plausible to suggest that a complex and integrated structure such as the wing appeared by an abrupt accident; it would have to be a gradual accumulation of accidents. Yet the fossil record has not revealed the series of intermediary stages; these are some of the many missing links. Fossils suggesting intermediary stages may indeed be there, lying undiscovered; or seemingly intermediary forms may have existed without being fossilised – so these missing links do not disprove chance evolution. But, when so much is missing, is anyone justified in saying that gradualism is the only hypothesis compatible with observation?

This objection is reinforced by the emergence of the debate between gradualists and punctuationists, a debate over the correct interpretation of the parts of the record that are *not* missing. Materialists will be quick to point out that even a punctuationalist account can be made to fit the chance-and-necessity thesis, because they claim that evolution has never been shown by punctuationalists to accelerate beyond the limit of what could plausibly be fuelled by a random supply of mutations. But the chance-and-necessity story has to work much harder here to be consistent with observations than the design hypothesis does.

An implicit aim of many biologists is to reduce the complete sphere of life — human, animal and vegetable — to physio-chemical reactions that obey the laws of physics. The claim that humans are simply physio-chemical machines is derived from such an aim. However, there is very little evidence to support this mechanistic and materialistic view of man. When so little is understood of biological and psychological phenomena, such a perspective requires a great leap of faith. Consider, for example, the remarkable emergence of consciousness in the higher forms of life. Descartes, in his partial materialism, asserted that animals are not, in fact, conscious. They are only machines, responding to stimuli. To him, an immaterial soul was a necessary condition for the experiences we encounter in our mental life. Since he considered animals to be without souls, he and his followers felt no qualms about performing vivisections in furtherance of their anatomical research. This was a way of reconciling materialism with the fact of consciousness. Following his objective to reduce as much of the world as he could to the laws of the emerging new physics, Descartes asserted that in animal behaviour there is no more than what we see: a physical stimulus (such as the penetration of tissue by a scalpel) and events in a physical body (such as the production of piercing noises in the animal's vocal chords). In animals, he argued, there is no feeling of pain, because there is no mental life. Present-day materialists do not have such an easy way of dispensing with consciousness, because they include human beings just as wholly in the material world as they do animals. Their thesis is that somehow, in both animals and humans, consciousness developed by chance — a phenomenon produced and controlled by brain cells programmed through chromosomes to manufacture this or that protein in response to this or that stimulus. Far from being a tested fact, this assertion is sheer speculation. How could we ever test the theory that chemicals might produce consciousness? No one has yet conceived of how this could be done.

Karl Popper points to the logical possibility that a complete theoretical understanding of life might be impossible to achieve in physical terms:

> There may be no theoretical reduction of biology to physics, just as there seems to be neither a theoretical reduction of mechanics to electrodynamics, nor a theoretical reduction the other way round.
>
> If the situation is such that, on the one hand, living organisms may originate by a natural process from non-living systems, and that, on the other hand, there is no complete theoretical understanding of life possible in physical terms, then we might speak of life as an emergent property of physical bodies, or of matter.
>
> Now I want to make it quite clear that as a rationalist I wish and hope to understand the world and that I wish and hope for a reduction. At the same time, I think it quite likely that there may be no reduction possible; it is conceivable that life is an emergent property of physical bodies.[14]

Arthur Koestler has summed up the views of many scholars who are dissatisfied with too glib a reduction of pyschology and biology to physics:

> There is 'an undercurrent of thought in the minds of perhaps hundreds of biologists', who are critical of the totalitarian claims of the neo-Darwinian orthodoxy; who refuse to believe that the so-called Synthetic Theory provides all the answers to the problems posed by the phenomena of evolution; and who feel that the theory reflects part of the picture but not the whole picture. Such critical tendencies are also in evidence in other life sciences, from genetics to psychology. There is, for instance, a growing conviction among psychologists that the behaviourists' . . . schema of chained responses, for all its historical merits, is changing from a once useful tool into an impediment to future progress. The common target . . . seems to be . . . the

robotomorphic view of man, or more soberly the insufficient emancipation of the life sciences from the mechanistic concepts of the nineteenth-century physics, and the resulting crudely reductionist philosophy.[15]

Constantly looking to physics to provide natural explanations for living systems may not ultimately help the biologist. Given the current radical nature of modern physics, it can only confirm the fact that the operation of life is mysterious and not at all understood. In fact, modern physics will discourage the biologist from making any such reduction and will suggest that there may be fundamental limitations to the 'tools' of biology. Biologists may be looking for natural causes in all phenomena as a reaction to the religious dogma of the past and not due to any scientific reason.

An alternative to materialism

There is an alternative to the materialist model that is not creationist. It does not reject the fact of evolution and, with respect, whatever Jacques Monod may insist to the contrary, it is a conceivable hypothesis, compatible with observed and tested fact. This is the hypothesis that some of those evolutionary events that the modern synthesis counts as accidents – the occurrence of genetic mutations leading to new forms of life – are not accidents but changes that appear by design, determined by a force outside nature itself. According to this view, new forms of life that have survived did not just happen to appear where conditions happened to favour them; these conditions were meant to be, and these forms of life were meant to flourish in them. Such a thesis accords better with our natural tendency to view living beings as goal-directed. It also fits more comfortably with the analogy of a computer program which is currently used in modern biology to explain the nature of the genetic code.

Biological structures are almost impossible to speak of without treating them as though made for a purpose. On meeting some unexplained piece of anatomy, such as the unique 'pot' on the nose of the male gharial, a crocodilian of the Indian subcontinent, a biologist invariably asks, what is this structure *for*? The mind is directed, in its search for explanatory hypotheses, towards the problems that a gharial faces in life, and towards their possible solutions. Perhaps the gharial faces problems in finding a mate which are unlike the problems of other crocodilians, and so this male crocodilian must be recognisably male from a distance. The fact that we are bound to think in this way is called the teleological paradox (from the Greek *telos* for 'end' in the sense of 'purpose'). It is a paradox because life is supposed to have no purpose, and the pot on the male gharial's nose is supposed to have developed accidentally and to have been kept in the species by an accidentally occurring necessity for it.

This paradox is implicit in the very analogy of the computer program by which we help our minds to picture the way that chromosomes control the functions of cells. Real-life computer programs are written not by accident but in order to produce intended results. Each of the millions upon millions of programs operating in nature to provide organisms with solutions to their life problems is on the face of it a piece of evidence for the existence of a *programmer*. Materialist approaches to biology provide one alternative to this way of seeing the evidence, often taking very complex and involved routes to their explanations of how biological programs could have come into being by an accumulation of accidents. They do not provide the only hypothesis compatible with the evidence, however.

The computer-program model for an organism's behaviour may be a good one, as evidenced by its success in molecular biology, but its extension to incorporate programs written accidentally is not a logical one. It is more logical to assume, given the genetic program model, that the development of a living system is due to the execution of a higher-level program, one that has been responsible for the development of the species itself. This would imply that events effecting changes in the genetic code would not all be as random as the modern synthesis supposes. Some of them would be teleological signals executing a program inherent in a world itself programmed to develop species. In other words, a living system, when developing to achieve its morphogenetic goals, may be running on a 'subroutine' of a much larger program, one that has directed the development of the species itself. To consider such a possibility is perfectly logical, much more so than inventing unnecessarily complicated models of accidentally created programs.

The implications of this proposal are that the development of species proceeds like that of a single living organism, in a highly organised, programmed way. The human species, for instance, may have passed through many stages of evolution, like the foetus in the womb of the mother – at one stage resembling a fish, at another an ape, and so on, while remaining essentially *human*. Thus the possibility exists that there is a teleological principle for the species itself, the origin of which is a separate question, but this does not detract from its overall feasibility.

The Model of Evolution Applied to Society

The strong secular movement which arose in the nineteenth century appealed to science as its source of guidance in overthrowing many long-cherished social and religious traditions. It served a great purpose, putting an end to many fallacious and superstitious dogmas. The movement, for instance, showed that literal interpretations of the Bible were not in agreement with scientific evidence and hence were a set of irrational dogmas that should not be taken seriously. But along with these dogmas, it rejected all religious doctrines and banished them from the emerging new society. This society was founded not only on scientific method, but also on anti-religious principles. That was, and still is, a mistake. Implictly woven into the foundation of today's secular society are an anti-religious spirit of nihilism and a belief in the animal nature of human beings. These two reductions are incapable of the objective, scientific justification claimed for them. Nevertheless, they characterise modern society.

Social determinism

The assumption that humans are simply animals has stimulated a search for material causes in the social sciences. The German revolutionary Karl Marx (1818–83) was an early admirer of Darwin and founded a 'scientific socialism'. He was also heavily influenced by G. W. F. Hegel (1770–1831), the German philosopher whose 'dialectics' of historical change taught that every historical epoch contains a self-contradiction, a seed of the events that will destroy the epoch and create a new one. Evolutionary theory struck Marx as supplying the model for a 'dialectical materialism'. In nature, new forms of life themselves change the natural environment and thereby create new ecological niches, to be filled with new forms of life which may replace old ones. In human history, said Marx, technological and economic changes bring into being new social classes which of necessity overthrow old ones. In the exclusively scientific spirit of the times, Marx saw all religious institutions as unconscious social adaptations of the ruling classes in their struggle to survive in a position of advantage: religion was the 'opiate of the people', promising them eternal rewards in return for obedience, thus dulling their anger at being exploited. Marx believed that political developments far into the future could be predicted by a scientific analysis of the necessary consequences of struggles between classes.

Many social scientists today would avoid speaking of laws of social change, because such laws have been so difficult to formulate; but a lack of predictive power in their discipline is seen only as a sign of its underdevelopment and of the complexity of its subject. The notion that human history may be unpredictable because humans have the free will to choose their path as they go is not taken into account, because we are seen as programmed robots. Social scientists have typically looked for the author of our behavioural programs in the accident of our environmental circumstances. Unlike animals born with complex instincts, a human's innate behavioural program is supposed to be limited to a tendency to recoil from pain and to seek pleasure. By regularly encountering pains and pleasures in the environment that they happen to be born into, people undergo a conditioning that fills in the rest of the program. By controlling the robot's pains and pleasures, society — its own structure determined by an ultimately accidental historical process — is supposed to type in the program like some great, unconscious operator at a computer terminal.

The jungle model
Social determinism is often characterised by the hope that the class conflicts that social accident and necessity engender will somehow produce a better society and a better human race. Other materialist

views of society have not been so optimistic and have come to embrace not only a survival philosophy but also a social pattern which is supposed to have dominated our evolution: the law of the jungle.

In the jungle, so the analogy runs, the struggle for survival is the dominant feature, and those qualities that lead to survival are the most important. Aggression, strength, power and competition are the qualities that prevail. Many of today's 'leaders' preach this philosophy, but today it is clearly more than a philosophy; it is a way of life. The functioning of human society has been modelled on the struggle for survival in the jungle. Today's society strives in all earnestness to acquire these jungle characteristics.

Simultaneous with the birth of Marxism, whole-hearted capitalists like the United States multimillionaire Andrew Carnegie (1835–1919) drew with equal enthusiasm from Spencer and Darwin to justify their obsessive race against business competitors. The capitalist ethic whereby competition weeds out the weakest elements of industrial society, ensuring survival only for the strongest and the most efficient, was elevated into a law of nature. This ethic continues to be dominant in many of the world's most industrialised countries.

Recently, in a spirit of pessimism about human moral progress, there has been a reaction among some academic researchers against social determinism. However, they have turned increasingly to biological determinism, which continues to command strong allegiance. The role of instinct is allowed to be much greater nowadays, and writers like Desmond Morris warn us not to make too much of civilisation, which is only a very recent influence on our character:

The human animal appears to have adapted brilliantly to his extraordinary new condition, but he has not had time to change biologically, to evolve into a new, genetically civilised species. This civilising process has been accomplished entirely by learning and conditioning. Biologically he is still the simple tribal animal . . . He lived like that, not for centuries, but for a million hard years. During that period he did change biologically. He evolved spectacularly. The pressures of survival were great and they moulded him.[16]

This way of thinking turns confidently to the animal world for models of behaviour by which to understand the human animal. If aggression and the struggle for dominance are found to be characteristic of social species of primates that have evolved in conditions similar to those conjectured for mankind's early development, then it is felt we too must be bound by these instincts and fundamentally incapable of loving peace or making the world one:

> The sobering lesson to be learnt . . . is that the ancient biological need of the human species for a distinct tribal identity is a powerful force that cannot be subdued. As fast as one super-tribal split is invisibly mended, another one appears. Well-meaning authorities talk airily about 'hopes for a global society'. They see clearly the technical possibility of such a development, given the marvels of modern communication, but they stubbornly overlook the biological difficulties.[17]

'Realism'

The effect of the survival philosophy, social determinism and the jungle model has been to give rise to a predominant belief in 'realism'. 'Realism' is the conviction that aggression, power struggles, class conflicts etc., are the most dominant factors at work in society. Most important of all, it is the justifying ethic of many political actions taken in the world today. It lies at the foundation of the military philosophy, a philosophy based on strength, supremacy and deterrence.

'Realism' in history goes under the name of 'objectivity'. Human history is interpreted as a series of power struggles, class conflicts and wars; in short, a history of survival. Moral values and religious beliefs are played down. Religious history is reduced to one of economics and politics. 'Objectivity' in history has come to mean the adoption of anti-religious axioms. The conflicts of religion and science are highlighted, and thus religion is seen as a hindrance to progress rather than the cause of it. In fact, mankind's complete history has been rewritten as a history of science and survival.

With the advent of today's 'realism', idealism has taken on a new definition. It is no longer the idealism defined by the past philosophers, representing the greater truth beyond the surface reality. It has come to mean everything that does not fit into the survival philosophy. While wars of history are invoked as examples of the innate aggression of human nature, goals based on unity, co-operation and amity are seen as unrealistic or hopelessly idealistic. Any goals that do not give a dominant role to our intrinsically aggressive, selfish nature are dismissed as unimportant.

World peace is seen as an idealistic notion, an unattainable goal. This belief is reflected in the military strategy of strength that today dominates the policies of nations. Peace negotiations are given a secondary role, while military strength and dominance are accorded primacy. The philosophy of deterrence epitomises this belief; only strength and military advantage will deter an enemy from attacking, and solutions to national conflicts ultimately lie with military supremacy. All the great sums of money and the vast amounts of human and national resources that are expended on the arms race are justified and underscored by this dogma of 'realism'. All these philosophies and actions have at their origin two fundamental axioms: that man is nothing but an animal and that there is no other purpose to life than survival.

The abuse of science and rejection of morality

Arising out of the major conflicts between science and religion in the nineteenth century, today's secular society is profoundly convinced of scientific truth and objective knowledge. The latter has become the sole criterion by which all phenomena must now be judged. This stance aims to create an objective, valueless society, but in practice it falls short and creates a society founded on anti-religious values. The tendency to look to science to explain all phenomena has led to serious difficulties; yet even now there are those who see science as the panacea for all the ills of the world. Science, on the contrary, has provided lethal weapons of destruction which are in the hands of wild animals who openly boast their willingness to use them if circumstances require it. It is one of the most dangerous contradictions of our time – the willingness to use weapons of global destruction for the objective of survival. Science has no intrinsic morality – nor is it essentially good or bad. It is a neutral tool, which can be used wisely or not.

In the analogy of the computer used earlier, where science represents the hardware and religion the software, the hardware (science) is given direction, organisation and purpose by the software (religion). The software that currently runs society, and consequently science, is based on chance and survival. It is software largely written in reactionary response to Christian dogmatism. Thus to look for morality from science is an abuse of science, and in practice science is largely used to serve anti-religious values. Far from providing a solution to the world's problems, at present science is being used to deepen them.

The propaganda put out in the name of science and objectivity may be likened to the dogma of the Catholic Church in the past. The Church had incorporated Greek astronomical conceptions into religious doctrine and imposed them on society at large, an action lacking any support in the Bible. Similarly the priests of the secular society – technocrats, biologists, etc. – have propagated anti-religious dogma in the name of science, and have used bad reductions as evidence to justify them. Their actions are unsupported by the principle of objectivity. They have, like the Catholic Church at the time of Galileo, abused and misused their own professed standards.

Any system or society needs initial starting conditions, axioms and values by which it can function. In former times religion, not science, provided these. Moral values have for the most part been derived from a religion in one form or another. The anti-religious beliefs that lie at the foundation of the modern secular society produce a society that deeply reflects them. It is not that every society intrinsically operates according to the principles of chance and survival, as the 'priests' of today would have us believe; rather, today's society has been fashioned and deliberately modelled to run this way.

Characteristic of chance is fragmentation, and it is under fragmented conditions that today's orderless society of specialists flourishes. Thus scientists can work on weapons of destruction and absolve themselves of any responsibility for how their work is used. Similarly, the consumer society is brainwashed into buying unhealthy, trivial products which it does not require, and a rampant industry can pollute the world's natural environment without regard to the long-term ecological destruction it causes. All is sacrificed for economic profit, which uses the premise of individual survival in its defence. The need to take individual moral responsibility for these actions is played down, as the 'survival machines' seek better ways to self-destruct.

The contradictions of survival

Mankind is beset with many seemingly intractable problems. We have reached a fundamental dichotomy. The need for world unity and world co-operation has become a paramount and dire necessity, the only course for survival; yet it is rejected out of hand as unrealistic, condemned as a utopian dream, a pious hope. Our response to the unprecedented global problems of today is paralysed by this contradiction. Underlying such a profound paralysis is the dogma of 'realism', which in turn emanates from the survival and jungle philosophies previously mentioned. This belief that human nature is nothing more than brute animal nature makes the problems of the world seem insurmountable. The materialistic philosophies of both the political right and the left have failed, serving only to polarise the world artificially and to create new problems. The confusion is deepened when the survival philosophy is given pseudo-scientific credence based on bad reductions. Yet the real source of the paralysis may have come from a fundamental course of action made in the nineteenth century, when religion was banished and replaced with anti-religious doctrines.

There are other contradictions that followers of the survival philosophy must contend with. One is that in our pursuit of individual survival we have reached a point where collective survival is threatened. We are approaching the antithesis of our goal of survival. 'The best for the individual part is gained by acquiring the best for the whole,' but the survival philosophy has created an aggressive, selfish society which is now balanced precariously on the brink of destruction. Is this not an indication that such a philosophy taken on its own is not enough? Another contradiction appears in the rejection of moral and religious values. The secular society refuses to accept such values, which are generally considered to be overtly 'subjective' and not directly amenable to objective analysis. But with the experience of living with the hazards of the global jungle, where the unacceptable elements of global aggression and dominance hold sway, society is clearly in dire need of the same moral values it previously rejected, those of trust, love, amity and faith: in short, religious values.

It is time to assess the fruits of the anti-religious foundation of modern secular society. What have been the results of such doctrines? One could venture to assert that the consequences have been extremely damaging; they have created a global super-jungle in which the principles of chance and survival provide an inadequate and defective basis for human society. One of the most damaging effects of these doctrines has been to extinguish hope and joy in society and render it powerless to respond to the many global challenges now facing mankind. Society must acknowledge the failures of these doctrines before it can act with fresh resolve to find better ones. It must replace chance and survival with design and purpose, but its new vision must be broad – one that encompasses all aspects of human nature and not just the animal part, one that reaches towards a higher transcendental purpose and not just the modest one of staying alive.

A New Model of Evolution and Design

There are a number of alternative conceptions of human evolution which have been variously advanced against the materialistic perspective, chance and survival. The model that is presented in this section is based on the author's understanding of the Bahá'í writings on the subject. Much fuller discussions of the Bahá'í approach can be found, but it may be of interest to include a summary of it here.[18]

The human spirit

The Bahá'í writings propose the existence of a human spirit, an immortal, indivisible, transcendental entity that in part makes up the human condition (and in Western theology is termed the soul). Human beings, it is asserted, are made up of an animal or bodily part as well as the human spirit. The latter is, however, independent of the body and has the same relationship to it that the sun has to a mirror that is held up to reflect its light. The mirror may be shattered, but the sun continues to shine; the body may be damaged or destroyed, but the human spirit will continue to exist. The human spirit is the source of the mind and intellect, which distinguish humans from animals. This spirit can train its powers on purely material things, or reflect upon the divine – depending on the use of the free will with which the human race is endowed.

The Bahá'í writings explain that human purpose in this world is to acquire divine or spiritual attributes. This is done by educating the human spirit in divine qualities, which are revealed to us through the prophets and holy books. The human spirit is given to us for precisely this reason; it is the means by which we progress spiritually. The illumination or cultivation of the human spirit by divine guidance helps us achieve our second purpose in life, namely to carry forward an ever-advancing civilisation. This civilisation is both divine and material. The human spirit is thus the vehicle of our progress both materially and spiritually. If, however, it is deprived of spiritual guidance and we turn wholly to the material side of our nature, then we become more savage, more cruel than any animal; we become super-animals, capable of much more destruction than any ordinary beast. Thus the human spirit must at all times receive divine guidance, but whether or not we choose to follow this guidance depends on our own free will.

'Abdu'l-Bahá, in explaining the nature of the human spirit, stated:

> The human spirit which distinguishes man from the animal is the rational soul; and these two names – the human spirit and the rational soul – designate one thing. This spirit, which in the terminology of the philosophers is the rational soul, embraces all beings, and as far as human ability permits discovers the realities of things and becomes cognisant of their peculiarities and effects, and of the qualities and properties of beings. But the human spirit, unless assisted by the spirit of faith, does not become acquainted with the divine secrets and the heavenly realities. It is like a mirror which, although clear, polished and brilliant, is still in need of light. Until a ray of the sun reflects upon it, it cannot discover the heavenly secrets.
>
> But the mind is the power of the human spirit. Spirit is the lamp; mind is the light which shines from the lamp. Spirit is the tree, and the mind is the fruit. Mind is the perfection of the spirit and its essential quality, as the sun's rays are the necessity of the sun. [19]

Elsewhere he describes the connection between the human spirit and the body:

> Therefore, it is evident and certain that the spirit is different from the body, and that its duration is independent of that of the body; on the contrary, the spirit with the utmost greatness rules in the world of the body; and its power and influence, like the bounty of the sun in the mirror, are apparent and visible. But when the mirror becomes dusty or breaks, it will cease to reflect the rays of the sun.[20]

The human spirit as defined in the Bahá'í writings is not material or tangible, yet when it is cultivated by divine qualities it is the sole cause of our spiritual and material development. It cannot be reduced to an entity that is housed in the brain or body, no more than the sun can be put in a mirror. It is, however, the noble part of human nature, the hallmark that distinguishes us from other forms of life on earth. The animal part is not intrinsically evil, but should be subservient to the human spirit. The Bahá'í writings state that the animal and vegetable worlds also have a transcendental nature, a particular spirit of their own, but their spirit is not as highly evolved as the human spirit. The human being cannot be reduced to the animal any more than the animal can be reduced to the vegetable or the vegetable to the mineral. They are intrinsically different, transcendentally different. Therefore, it is not possible to reduce all life forms into mechanistic models based on the mineral or material world. To say that the human being is purely an animal is equivalent to denying the existence of the human spirit, since the human spirit carries with it our central purpose. The unfortunate consequence of this distortion of the human character is that it may retard spiritual progress, and emphasise man's animal nature and anti-social qualities.

'Abdu'l-Bahá confirms that, were we to model ourselves on the animal alone, conflict and strife would result; the only way out of this condition is to acquire divine education:

> In the world of nature the dominant note is the struggle for existence – the result of which is the survival of the fittest. The law of the survival of the fittest is the origin of all difficulties. It is

the cause of war and strife, hatred and animosity, between human beings. In the world of nature there is tyranny, egoism, aggression, overbearance, usurpation of the rights of others and other blameworthy attributes which are defects of the animal world. Therefore, so long as the requirements of the natural world play paramount part among the children of men, success and prosperity are impossible.[21]

The evolution of the human species

The Bahá'í Faith categorically affirms the phenomenon of the evolution of life on earth, but states that evolution has been designed and is not the outcome of blind chance. In the words of 'Abdu'l-Bahá:

> Moses taught that the world was brought into existence in the six days of creation. This is an allegory, a symbolic form of the ancient truth that the world evolved gradually. Darwin can refer to Moses for his theory of evolution. God did not allow the world to come into existence all at once, rather the divine breath of life manifested itself in the commanding Word of God, *Logos,* which engendered and begot the world. We thus have a progressive process of creation, and not a one-time happening. Moses' days of creation represent time spans of millions of years. From Pythagoras to ibn-i-Síná (known as Avicenna) to the 'faithful brothers from Basra', through Darwin and to the blessed manifestations of the Báb and Bahá'u'lláh, both scholars and Prophets have testified to the progressive creative action of the *Logos* (divine breath of life). The Darwinian and monistic theories of evolution and the origin of species are not materialistic, atheistic ideas; they are religious truths which the godless and the deluded have unjustifiably used in their campaign against religion and the Bible.[22]

This perspective of the evolution of humanity may be understood with the help of some analogies. One is that the human species developed like the seed of a tree. From the moment it is planted in the ground the seed undergoes different stages of development through the passage of time. The seed of the tree, however, is distinct and different from the seeds of other plants from the very beginning, even though there may have been a time when other seeds physically resembled it. Hence in the same way it is stated in the Bahá'í writings that man developed as a distinct species and was not derived from any other species. The growth rates of different species obviously varied, like the growth rates of different plants, but the fact that the species of man came to fruition directly after certain other species does not necessarily mean that it was derived from them.

Another way to view the evolution of the human species is to liken it to the evolution of a foetus in the womb of the mother. Although the foetus passes through many different phases of evolution and thus may appear to resemble a member of a different species at a particular stage, it always belongs to one distinct species, following one continuous line of development. Similarly, the human species evolved through different phases. At one stage it may have resembled a fish, at another an ape, but all the way through its evolution it was a distinct species undergoing a process of design. It is important to note that the environment also plays a part; a plant must be nurtured and looked after if it is to grow up to be healthy. Hence man's development can be attributed to two factors; one has been the operation of a teleological principle, a genetic design, the other has been the influence of environmental conditions, as assumed in orthodox biological theory. 'Abdu'l-Bahá describes this process:

As man in the womb of the mother passes from form to form, from shape to shape, changes and develops, and is still the human species from the beginning of the embryonic period — in the same way man, from the beginning of his existence in the matrix of the world, is also a distinct species — that is, man — and has gradually evolved from one form to another. Therefore, this change of appearance, this evolution of members, this development and growth, even though we admit the reality of growth and progress, does not prevent the species from being original.[23]

A genetic program for the development of the species is just one possible analogy; it is by no means the only one which could express the idea of a teleological principle in the evolution of the human species. Some writers have spoken of morphogenetic fields, which not only guide the development of an individual organism but also that of a species, and of temporal fields based on 'biological clocks'.[24]

Social and spiritual evolution

The Bahá'í account of evolution does not stop at the biological evolution of the human species. It asserts that mankind has evolved intellectually, culturally and spiritually under the same principle of designed evolution that guided his physical development. A teleological principle, ultimately spiritual in character, has taken man through his different phases of cultural evolution. The goal of this progressive development has been and still is to carry forward an ever-advancing civilisation, a civilisation which advances through the acquisition of divine attributes and not purely material ones.

The Bahá'í Faith explains that the development of the human spirit has also been in accordance with this grand principle of designed evolution. Thus the intellectual faculty of man gradually evolved through both the influence of divine guidance (through prophets and their holy books) and the operation of a teleological principle on man's mental faculty. The social and spiritual history of mankind may be seen as one of natural organic growth, which has been carefully nurtured into its present state by a succession of spiritual luminaries. The claim is that cultural progress has developed in accordance with a design, and human society has passed through determined stages, all of which have had religion at their foundation. Religion is progressively revealed to man in order to take him to higher stages of spiritual development, a process which is never-ending. This means that all the major religions of the past ultimately come from the same source and were revealed for the same purpose; that of educating mankind in divine principles.

The evolution of mankind may be compared to the different growing periods of an individual human being. Just as the individual passes through the stages of infancy, childhood, adolescence and adulthood, 'Abdu'l-Bahá explains that humanity has also passed through these successive stages and is now at the threshold of maturity:

From the beginning to the end of his life man passes through certain periods or stages each of which is marked by certain conditions peculiar to itself. For instance during the period of childhood his conditions and requirements are characteristic of that degree of intelligence and capacity. After a time he enters the period of youth in which his former conditions and needs are superseded by new requirements applicable to the advance in his degree. His faculties of observation are broadened and deepened, his intelligent capacities are trained and awakened, the limitations and environment of childhood no longer restrict his energies and accomplishments. At last he passes out of the period of youth and enters the stage or station of maturity which necessitates another transformation and corresponding advance in his sphere of life-activity. New powers and perceptions clothe him, teaching and training commensurate with his progression occupy his mind, special bounties and bestowals descend in proportion to his increased capacities and his former period of youth and its conditions will no longer satisfy his matured view and vision.

Similarly there are periods and stages in the life of the aggregate world of humanity, which at one time was passing through its degrees of childhood, at another its time of youth but now has entered its long presaged period of maturity, the evidences of which are everywhere visible and apparent. Therefore the requirements and the conditions of former periods have changed and merged into exigencies which distinctly characterise the present age of the world of mankind. That which was applicable to human needs during the early history of the race could neither meet nor satisfy the demands of this day and period of newness and consummation. Humanity has emerged from its former degrees of limitation and preliminary training. Man must now become imbued with new virtues and powers, new moralities, new capacities . . .

From every standpoint the world of humanity is undergoing a re-formation. The laws of former governments and civilisations are in a process of revision, scientific ideas and theories are developing and advancing to meet a new range of phenomena, invention and discovery are penetrating hitherto unknown fields revealing new wonders and hidden secrets of the material universe; industries have vastly wider scope and production; everywhere the world of mankind is in the throes of evolutionary activity indicating the passing of the old conditions and advent of the new age of re-formation. Old trees yield no fruitage; old ideas and methods are obsolete and worthless now. Old standards of ethics, moral codes and methods of living in the past will not suffice for the present age of advancement and progress.[25]

Thus according to the Bahá'í Faith the present upheavals in the world of humanity may be likened to the turbulent period of an adolescent who is struggling to assume the responsibilities of an adult. In his efforts to attain adulthood, self-realisation and independence he has rejected all previous guidance, rebelled against his former life-style and is now caught between two worlds; that of youth and that of the adult. The characteristic features of a youth reaching maturity are agitation, insecurity, rebellion and unrest. Likewise the conflicts of war, aggression and fanaticism in the world today may be seen as immature expressions of an agitated humanity's desperate struggle for maturity. Within this context, the nineteenth-century rejection of religion and the rise of today's secular society represent an act of rebellion and a transitory phase of evolution. The former ideologies and institutions of humanity, although once invaluable to its progress, are now hopelessly deficient. We have reached a unique stage in our evolution, and insistence on outworn ideologies and institutions today retards our progress and delays our attainment of maturity. The Bahá'í writings indicate that mankind is rapidly approaching the highest stage of its evolution on this planet, a stage of maturity which will be characterised by the attainment of lasting world peace and unity. Shoghi Effendi, the Guardian of the Bahá'í Faith, stated:

Unification of the whole of mankind is the hall-mark of the stage which human society is now approaching. Unity of family, of tribe, of city-state, and nation have been successively attempted and fully established. World unity is the goal towards which a harassed humanity is striving. Nation-building has come to an end. The anarchy inherent in state sovereignty is moving towards a climax. A world growing to maturity must abandon this fetish, recognise the oneness and wholeness of human relationships, and establish once for all the machinery that can best incarnate this fundamental principle of its life.[26]

Humanity may be likened to a seemingly ill patient. The doctors who surround the patient may represent today's worldly wise, who have prescribed the various cures of capitalism, socialism, 'freedom', the survival philosophy and so on, for the patient. These cures, rather than leading to recovery, have further aggravated the illness, and have added to the patient's suffering. The doctors have concluded that mankind is on the verge of dying; the spasms of terrorism, fanaticism and war grow daily. However, the convulsions of pain and suffering that attack the body of mankind may be thought of as labour pains that are now rapidly approaching the climactic discharge of a new world order. The rupturing and tearing down of the old ties of military nationalism, racism and religious bigotry are some of the necessary preparations for this discharge. The human race is undergoing a social and spiritual birth, one, it is claimed, that was conceived through the vibrating influence of the latest divine revelation to man, which the Bahá'í Faith claims to be:

> We stand on the threshold of an age whose convulsions proclaim alike the death-pangs of the old order and the birth-pangs of the new. Through the generating influence of the Faith announced by Bahá'u'lláh this New World Order may be said to have been conceived. We can, at the present moment, experience its stirrings in the womb of a travailing age — an age waiting for the appointed hour at which it can cast its burden and yield its fairest fruit.[27]

Our greatest challenge

It is not the purpose of this book to give a detailed picture of the Bahá'í conception of the future evolution of mankind. This may be found elsewhere,[28] and only a basic description is relevant here. According to the Bahá'í view, the greatest challenge now facing mankind is the establishment of world peace, and the subsequent development of an organic world civilisation, a necessary step if the rights and interests of every member of the human race are to be secured.

The first stage in this process of social evolution must be the signing of a lasting, binding agreement of collective security which will mark the cessation of war. All the nations of the world must participate in its deliberations, and the treaty must be binding on every country and enjoy universal support. Initially, such an agreement will be brought about and maintained through the force of practical necessity, of survival, but it will provide the foundation for a more mature and far-reaching peace. Only on this basis can the unity of mankind be realised, and a world civilisation, founded on spiritual principles, be fully and permanently established. However, this second stage in the social evolution of the human race could take centuries to complete. The essential components of a future world community are multifarious:

the inevitable curtailment of unfettered national soverignty as an indispensable preliminary to the formation of the future Commonwealth of all the nations . . . Some form of a world Super-State must needs be evolved, in whose favour all the nations of the world will have willingly ceded every claim to make war, certain rights to impose taxation and all rights to maintain armaments, except for purposes of maintaining internal order within their respective dominions. Such a state will have to include within its orbit an International Executive adequate to enforce supreme and unchallengeable authority on every recalcitrant member of the commonwealth; a World Parliament whose members shall be elected by the people in their respective countries and whose election shall be confirmed by their respective governments; and a Supreme Tribunal whose judgement will have a binding effect even in such cases where the parties concerned did not voluntarily agree to submit their case to its consideration. A world community in which all economic barriers will have been permanently demolished and the interdependence of Capital and Labour definitely recognised; in which the clamour of religious fanaticism and strife will have been forever stilled; in which the flame of racial animosity will have been finally extinguished; in which a single code of international law – the product of the considered judgement of the world's federated representatives – shall have as its sanction the instant and coercive intervention of the combined forces of the federated units; and finally a world community in which the fury of a capricious and militant nationalism will have been transmuted into an abiding consciousness of world citizenship – such indeed, appears, in its broadest outline, the Order anticipated by Bahá'u'lláh, an Order that shall come to be regarded as the fairest fruit of a slowly maturing age.[29]

This will not, however, be a unity based on uniformity; nor will it mean the existence of an excessively centralised authority. The individual autonomy and cultural identity of each nation will be respected and upheld. Underpinning such a commonwealth will be the principle of the oneness of mankind, and the protection of the interests of both the individual and society, and not one at the expense of the other. From the Bahá'í standpoint, world peace is not a possibility but an inevitability, and a vitally essential stage in the evolution of our planet. Whether it will be established through a series of catastrophic calamities as a result of nations clinging to age old prejudices such as nationalism and racism, or whether it will come about through constructive visionary acts of international consultation, remains to be seen.[30]

Global problems require global solutions. Only the erection of a universally accepted system of global controls can solve the unprecedented problems mankind faces in this era. Only a world government can legislate the laws required to regulate an organically interdependent world community. Only a world govenment can provide the much-needed world authority over and above national sovereignty. The world needs an economic system serving the interests of all mankind rather than a small, rich minority. It needs a framework within which technological development and scientific research are directed to humanitarian ends such as health, communication and the eradication of hunger, not directed to serving military organisations which seek national dominance and threaten world survival. The world needs to preserve its natural environment, the atmosphere, forests and rivers, instead of allowing their wholesale pollution by a rampant, short-sighted, profit-seeking industry. It needs an effective world judicial system, a forum to solve international grievances and disputes peacefully, instead of abandoning such a process to international terrorism and violence. While these ideals are widely shared, what is not recognised is the necessity for an international agency or world government to ensure their realisation. Without such a system, these goals may indeed be regarded as hopeless ideals and unrealistic dreams, rather than the practical requirements of a healthy and progressive global society.

In order to achieve world peace, the human race will undoubtedly find it necessary to reassess a number of prejudices and preconceptions. Among the first to be relinquished must be the belief in our fundamentally selfish and aggressive nature. Such a belief represents a gross distortion of the human character, and does not take into account our distinguishing feature: the human spirit. The despairing picture of man as a biological robot, an accidental prodigy of the ape family, devoid of free will and purpose, will surely fail to inspire humanity with the confidence to respond to the challenges of this age. Until we acknowledge our true nature and purpose, the human race may continue to suffer a paralysis of will, a hopelessness, and remain powerless to cope with today's global problems and rise to the challenge of securing peace in the world.

3. THE MEETING OF TWO WAYS

'How resplendent the luminaries of knowledge that shine in an atom, and how vast the oceans of wisdom that surge within a drop!'
Bahá'u'lláh

In the twentieth century there has been a new scientific revolution, and the theatre of events has once again been physics. This new revolution has yet to achieve its full social impact, and its philosophical spirit has not yet penetrated the whole scientific community; many biologists, in particular, remain unaffected by it. Eminent physicists openly confess the incomprehensibility of the rapid changes called for by the new physics in our understanding of matter and the universe, and it suggests such radical departures from previously held beliefs that some have even looked for anticipations of these new trends in the wisdom of ancient religions such as Buddhism and Taoism.[1] In this chapter we will consider some remarkable insights expressed in the teachings of one of the world's newest religions, the Bahá'í Faith, noting that the tone of the new physics points dramatically towards a harmony between the scientific and the spiritual. Let us begin with a sketch of developments in the twentieth-century laboratory.

New Horizons of the Material Realm

The pre-revolutionary philosophy that still pervades our society is inherent in Galileo's distinction between 'objective' primary properties and 'subjective' secondary ones. The objective properties of things are all supposed to be measurable in a way that leaves out the observer and the peculiarities of his subjective point of view. This should yield a single set of determinate truths about material reality, a reality that might be reduced to a model resembling some great piece of Renaissance machinery, a clock ticking away on its own according to the only pattern possible — the one made necessary by the arrangement of its wheels and the tension in its spring.

To seek a reduction is, of course, not a bad thing in science. It need amount to no more than raising the question as to whether an explanation of certain natural phenomena may be possible in terms of other, more easily comprehensible natural phenomena. There arose a tendency in the course of the first scientific revolution, however, to insist that there must in principle always be a reduction, and to insist that it must always reduce phenomena to a model that will make all things unmysterious and place them as surely within our grasp as clock wheels and springs. This tendency is known as 'reductionism', and the new physics has found it severely limiting. We have moved on to another conception of what it means to get a grip on reality.

The old subjective–objective distinction has been drastically modified. We are forced nowadays to acknowledge that measurements of time and space are relative to frames of reference and to admit that certain of our measurements must affect the very reality we are measuring. A principle of complementarity has had to be introduced, allowing equal weight to seemingly contradictory observations and incompatible approaches. Mathematical regularity in nature has been found to be not of the clockwork kind. The models now proposed both for the unseen world of atomic and subatomic particles and for the vast regions of intergalactic space are impossible to comprehend in terms of anything so familiar as the Renaissance invention ticking on the mantelshelf here in our own restricted slice of the cosmos. The mechanistic model, whatever its usefulness in originally making a scientific method possible, now seems wrongly inspired, and the new way of probing the material outer limits does nothing to banish from the mind a sense of speculation about the immaterial. New theories of the dynamics of the universe see it not as a machine left running but as a growing, mysteriously interconnected structure, and many find it impossible not to see direction and design in its development.

Relativity – the unimaginable universe

Newton's physics assumes a fixed frame of reference. Time is absolute, and so is the endless space that houses all material objects. This absolute frame of reference is an extension of time and space as they appear to us in our everyday earthbound experience. Light travels in straight lines through Newtonian space; and, in obedience to the geometry standardised in ancient times by Euclid, if it meets no obstacle it carries on to infinity. Partial confirmation of the general theory of relativity devised by Einstein has shown that this extension of our own familiar surroundings bears little resemblance to reality on its grander scale.

A point of departure for a new way of seeing things was the Michelson–Morley experiment of 1887. Two United States physicists, A. A. Michelson and E. W. Morley, wanted to discover once and for all whether there is any such thing as the 'ether' – an invisible medium that was thought to exist in the spaces between observable matter, transmitting the waves of light and other forms of energy that travel from one to the other. They reasoned that, if there is an ether, a ray of light projected in the direction that the earth is moving should be slowed down slightly by going against the stream of ether wind flowing around the moving earth. A beam of light projected in the opposite direction should be slightly speeded up on account of being carried along in the flow. When they conducted their experiment, Michelson and Morley found no difference in the speed of light travelling in either direction, with the implication that either the earth was not moving or there is no ether wind.

For the German-born physicist Albert Einstein (1879–1955) the one indisputable fact established by the experiment was that the velocity of light is not affected by the motion of the earth. He reasoned that it must be constant regardless of the motion of any other body in the universe as well, and that all the laws of nature are the same for all systems that move uniformly relative to one another. This is the basis of Einstein's theory of special relativity, published in 1905. Although on the surface not a startling assertion, the theory requires a description of nature without assuming any absolute, stationary frame of reference, and this is a great departure.

Space itself cannot be a frame of reference, because it is just a relationship between things. If nothing is spatially related, then there is no such thing as space. If only one item existed, it would be quite impossible to say how much space it occupies, where in space it is or whether it is moving and in what direction; a body can have location and change of location only relative to other bodies. Similarly with time: time relations hold between events; if there are no distinct events, there is no time. The Newtonian conception of space as a potentially empty vessel existing for all time is an illusion, and the scientist who wants to describe nature in terms that are consistent for all systems in the universe must treat measurements of time and distance as relative to the systems in which the measurements are made.

From these axioms, and using a series of equations developed for another purpose by the Dutch physicist H. A. Lorentz (1853–1928), Einstein derived a number of counter-intuitive results. For example, events are more distant from each other in time the faster the object in which they occur is moving; a clock attached to any moving system runs slower than a clock that is stationary. This difference is not great enough to matter on an earthly scale. You may fly half-way round the world and back at 500 miles per hour and it may seem that the minute hand on your watch has not lost any time by comparison with the minute hand on the stay-at-home kitchen clock. But a trip deep into space and back at high enough speeds would return you to earth noticeably younger than your stay-at-home twin, if you had one.

Another relativity that Newton was not aware of is that of inertia, the resistance of a body to acceleration. Einstein showed that inertia increases with velocity. The increase becomes perceptible only at speeds close to that of light, and this was soon confirmed experimentally in particle physics, in which observations of particles travelling near the speed of light became commonplace during the twentieth century. An understanding of the relativity of mass led to Einstein's immensely important discovery of the relationship between mass and energy, expressed in the famous formula $E=mc^2$. Energy has mass. The sun, decaying radioactive particles and exploding nuclear bombs are all examples of the transformation of one type of energy into another.

Einstein's general theory of relativity, published in November 1915, generalises special relativity, stating that the laws of nature are the same for all systems regardless of their state of motion. He was able to meet certain objections to special relativity by showing that there is no way of distinguishing the motion produced by inertial forces from motion produced by gravitational force. This is called the equivalence principle.

The general theory's account of gravity is given in terms of a mathematically cogent but unpicturable space–time continuum. Gravitational fields, analogous to electromagnetic fields, accentuate the unpicturability by distorting this space–time continuum into something that can be related only very remotely to our experience of meeting objects on earth at times told by the clock on the mantelshelf. Light, far from travelling in straight lines, is bent by the gravitational fields that it travels through. Although gravity waves have not yet been detected, the bending of light as it passed near our own sun was first measured, and found to be as Einstein predicted, during a solar eclipse in 1919. The cumulative effect of the mass of the universe is to bend light over into a closed curve. Taking several hundreds of billions of years, a photon of light could return to its point of emission, and a man, if he could wait long enough and see far enough, could see the back of his head. Time is slowed by strong gravitational fields, with the result that a clock would run slower on the surface of the sun than it does on earth. Predicted space–time singularities, points of immense gravitation now known as black holes, have been found by astronomers. One analogy that has been suggested for those who want to picture Einstein's universe is that of an enormous soap bubble. The interior of the bubble is nothing at all, not even space and the irregular rippling surface of the bubble represents the space–time continuum. This surface must be conceived as containing specks of matter whose changing positions determine the bubble's constantly changing shape.

Particles and waves – a mysterious duality

We began the twentieth century with a picture in our minds of atoms that were like minute solar systems, each with a nucleus surrounded by óne or more electrons in orbit. Electrons were small hard spheres described by James Clerk Maxwell as 'the imperishable foundation stones of the universe'. For this first model of the atom, we did not borrow directly from objects made familiar to us by our everyday experience, but we did something very similar. For this atomic reality, on an infinitesimally smaller scale than our own, we used a picture we had long constructed of the reality only one astronomic step up from our own. And our first expectation was that the objects in that world would obey the same laws of Newtonian mechanics that we applied to the ones in ours and in our solar system. This picture of the atom was temporary, for a retreat from mechanical description towards mathematical abstraction was soon found necessary.

The first note in the call to a retreat was sounded in 1901 by the German physicist Max Planck (1858–1947). In that year he published his quantum theory, attempting to resolve a long-standing problem about variations in the amount of radiant energy given off by ideal heated bodies or surfaces called 'black bodies'. The energy varies with wavelength and temperature in a way that wave theories of energy were unable to account for. Planck found a mathematical equation that satisfied for the first time the results of black body experiments. However, the equation rested on the assumption that radiant energy is emitted not in unbroken waves but in discontinuous and measurable 'quanta', which were curiously like 'particles' of energy.

In 1905 Einstein generalised the quantum theory to all forms of radiant energy, including light, heat and X-rays, and used it to explain the 'photoelectric effect'. The traditional wave theory of light had been unable to explain why, when light falls on a metal plate, a shower of electrons is ejected by the plate, or why the shower is greater when the light is of a higher frequency (such as violet) and less intense when the light is of a lower frequency (such as red). Einstein deduced that light is not emitted in unbroken waves but in quanta of light that he called 'photons'. The effect of a photon striking an electron is analoguous to one billiard ball striking another; hence the shower of electrons from an illuminated plate. A photon's energy is proportional to the frequency of the light emitted; hence the variation in the intensity of the shower when the light varies in frequency.

There continue, however, to be phenomena involving light that can be explained only by the wave theory. For example, if light is shone through a pinhole onto a screen, it diffracts into a pattern of alternating bands of light and darkness in a way that is comparable to ocean waves bending and diverging on passing through the narrow mouth of a harbour. If two adjacent pinholes allow two of these diffraction patterns to meet, they behave just like two wave systems meeting in a pond. Bright stripes occur where two light waves reinforce each other, and dark stripes occur where the two waves interfere destructively – just as waves of water reinforce each other when the crest of one wave meets the crest of another, and destroy each other when crest meets trough. If light travels as individual photons, and also displays these wave effects, then it would follow that somehow a single photon has some kind of 'knowledge' of the paths of preceding photons and finds its way to the right point in the pattern on the screen.

Light thus displays a very mysterious duality. In 1923 the French physicist Louis de Broglie proposed that the same strange duality can be found in matter. He deduced that electrons can display wavelike properties. Shortly afterwards the Austrian physicist Erwin Schrödinger (1887–1961) developed this idea in a highly abstract mathematical form that explained quantum phenomena by attributing specific wave functions to protons and electrons. This system is known as wave mechanics. It was experimentally confirmed when electrons were diffracted through crystals like X-ray waves.

To this paradoxical state of affairs the German physicist W. K. Heisenberg (1901–76) introduced the famous principle of uncertainty. He suggested that there is a fundamental limit on the measurement of minute entities, because observation is a function not only of the object under observation but also of the observer. The position and the momentum of a particle, for example, cannot both be measured with accuracy at the same time. If the position is measured, the momentum must be left uncertain. If the momentum is measured, the position must be left uncertain. An implication of Heisenberg's uncertainty principle is that we cannot *determine* whether light or matter is made up of particles or waves. The way we conduct any of the possible tests so affects the object of the test as to make it appear wavelike or like a particle. Physics has been forced to accept both the wave theory and its seeming contradiction, the particle theory, as complementary ways of describing reality.

Schrödinger's highly mathematical wave mechanics predicts and explains atomic phenomena with remarkable success, but it is extremely difficult to interpret in physical terms. The wave function can assume many different states. In 1926 a fundamental interpretation of the wave function was decided upon by a group of workers including as its central figure the Danish physicist Niels Bohr (1885–1962). Known as the 'Copenhagen interpretation', it sees the wave function as representing a probability. After a measurement is made the wave function collapses to one state which is partly determined by the method of observation. This radical view was never accepted by Einstein, who said in a letter to Bohr: 'I cannot believe that God plays dice with the world.'

An illustration in familiar terms of the bizarre nature of the Copenhagen interpretation was given by Schrödinger in 1935. Consider a cat in a box which also contains a bottle of poisonous gas. Imagine that the lid of the bottle can be opened by a completely random atomic event (a Geiger counter detects the event and triggers a release). The chance of the event occurring is 50 per cent, and so the cat has a 50 per cent chance of living or dying. The Copenhagen interpretation of Schrödinger's equation is comparable to an assertion that both possibilities exist, the cat's being alive and the cat's being dead, before the box is opened to see what happened. The cat is in a state of limbo before it is observed. Only by making the observation do we force one of these states to be real.

The EPR paradox

Einstein and two colleagues, B. Podolsky and N. Rosen, devised a thought experiment, which came to be known as the EPR experiment, to attempt to disprove the quantum mechanical paradox. A step had been taken in 1928 by the English physicist Paul Dirac to combine quantum mechanics and special relativity. The resulting 'Dirac equation' is now the standard equation underlying most particle physics. It shows that particles have an intrinsic spin, and that for certain particles (e.g. electrons) the spin can take only two forms, up or down if the measuring instrument is aligned vertically, left or right if the measuring instrument is aligned horizontally. What is described here is a version of the EPR experiment, similar to that presented by the English physicist David

Bohm. It is a modification of the original experiment, and is conceptually simpler than the original which dealt with the conservation of momentum and measurement of position. The EPR experiment imagines that two particles of this type, A and B, are emitted in opposite directions from an event, and they are observed when they have travelled some distance. Particle A when measured for vertical spin can either have spin up or spin down, or if the measurement is made in the horizontal direction, it will have spin left or spin right. The spin will align itself to the axis of measurement, but the precise spin state that a single particle has cannot be known in advance. It turns out that vertical spins and horiztonal spins are related to Heisenberg's uncertainty principle and that measuring the vertical spin with infinite precision rules out the possibility of knowing whether the horizontal spin is left or right.

Now consider an event which produces a 50 per cent chance of an up or a down spin. It happens that there is a law of spin conversion: if particle A is measured to have spin down, then particle B must have spin up. By Heisenberg's uncertainty principle, nothing can be deduced about the particle's horizontal spin state. If the measuring device is now orientated axially and measures in the horizontal direction, say, spin right for particle A, then particle B must have spin left (by spin conversion). But then the question arises: how did particle B know that it should switch from spin up, with uncertainty in its horizontal spin, to spin left when the measurement device was reorientated such a long distance away? Even more perplexing, if the measuring system were reorientated during the flight-time of the particles, this could mean that some form of non-local connection exists between the particles which is somehow dependent on the way they are measured.[2] Einstein stated that, if quantum mechanics were true, then the EPR experiment shows that it would violate the principle of local causes. Since this principle lies at the foundation of all physics, Einstein rejected the validity of quantum mechanics. Indeed, it would imply that somehow even if particles were to travel light-years apart there would be some mysterious form of coupling between them.

Contrary to Einstein's assertion, however, recent experiments have shown quantum mechanics to be correct. In 1964 John Bell devised a test for quantum mechanics which consisted of measuring the correlations of the spins of particle pairs, of the type already described. He devised a test called the 'Bell inequality', that would be violated if particle spins are correlated in accordance to the laws of quantum mechanics but would not be violated if the spins are uncorrelated as in the case of classical physics. Later experiments carried out by J. Clauser and S. Freedman (1972) or more recently by Alan Aspect (1982) show convincingly that Bell's inequality is indeed violated and by amounts that are predicted by quantum mechanics. However, there is a growing controversy among physicists over the type of non-locality that violation of Bell's inequality allows. Some would suggest that 'communication' is only exhibited in the cross-correlation of information on the two particles (i.e. a relationship becomes apparent only when comparing measurements of the particles), and hence this does not represent conclusive evidence for a violation of locality in a real or conventional sense. Others state that the experiment disproves the existence of 'hidden' local causes and thus inevitably implies the existence of non-local connections. The notion of reality has also been brought into question. Some physicists point out that there is another alternative to concluding that reality is non-local, and that is to state that reality does not exist until it is observed. It is obviously far too early to decide whether quantum mechanics really does imply the existence of non-local causes. It may indeed turn out that quantum mechanics is incomplete as stated by Einstein but, whatever the outcome, many physicists are convinced that the key to further advancement in physics lies in a proper understanding of its apparent paradoxes. To speculate about them at the present time, however, would be presumptious.

Antimatter and ghost particles

Solutions to the Dirac equation have yielded new, negative energy states. In order to avoid saying that particles lose their energy and fall into an abyss of negative energy, Dirac proposed that these negative energies were already occupied by electrons that are positively charged. A picture gradually emerged of two particle worlds, symmetrical to each other. The particles that occupy negative energy states were interpreted to be 'anti-particles', the anti-particle of an electron being called a positron. Not only has existence of anti-particles been confirmed experimentally, but anti-particles are accumulated and generated as standard experimental material for particle accelerators in high-energy physics. Antimatter and matter can mutually annihilate, liberating energy in the process. The amount of energy liberated is given by Einstein's mass-energy equivalence relation. The converse is also true; if a suitable amount of energy is contained in a small region of space, then matter and antimatter can be produced in equal amounts. This process is called pair production.

Recent work has shown that vacuums are filled with a continual production and annihilation of particles, an effect predicted by quantum mechanics, since time and energy are subject to Heisenberg's uncertainty principle. If an observation is made in a very short time, then the uncertainty in the energy range is very high; and since energy is equivalent to mass, it can be predicted that particle pairs are generated in these short times, an infinite variety of pairs being constantly created and destroyed. They are termed 'virtual' or 'ghost' particles, and a possible confirmation of their existence occurred in an experiment performed by M. J. Sparnay in 1958. The result of this experiment is known as the 'Casimir effect'. A residual electromagnetic force was detected in a chamber made free of matter by pumping and free of radiation by cooling. The area of study which developed from this result is known as 'stochastic electrodynamics'.

Messenger particles and unified field theory

Progress in science has always consisted in finding a way of bringing more and more data within the scope of fewer and fewer explanations. New theories overtake old ones because the scope of the old ones is found to be too restricted, and the constant dream of science is to have a single theory that can give a unified and coherent description of nature. Physicists see this hoped-for theory as a 'grand unified field theory', one that will explain how the fundamental forces of nature – the different types of field – are interrelated. It is believed by many that a successful theory may soon emerge and that it will relate certain particles thought to be closely associated with ghost particles. These are extremely short-lived particles of no fixed mass, the 'messenger' particles, so called because they are constantly emitted and absorbed by particles that they link. There are four types of messenger particle, each associated with one of nature's four fundamental forces and a major division in the study of physics:

1 *'Gravitons'* are the messenger particles thought to generate the gravitational force. They would seem to lie at the root of the phenomenon that Newton dealt with in his universal theory of gravitation and that Einstein probed more deeply in his general theory of relativity. A new approach called 'quantum gravity' attempts to apply quantum mechanics in understanding gravity. This work is as yet purely theoretical and has not produced any one particular theory.

2 *'Photons'* are the messenger particles for the electromagnetic force, which was comprehensively described by James Clerk Maxwell in the mid-nineteenth century. His theory successfully reduced the electrical field to the magnetic field and vice versa, uniting as one force what had previously been considered two. Quantum electrodynamics arose in the 1930s and has had great success in applying quantum mechanics to electromagnetic phenomena.

3 Plus and minus *'W-particles'* are associated with the 'weak' force, which is involved in the emission of an electron in radioactive decay and is present only in the nucleus of the atom. The first successful model to give a unified account of any of the four forces was proposed by S. Weinberg and A. Salam in 1969. This theory, known as the 'electroweak theory', combines the electromagnetic force and the weak force. It was experimentally confirmed in 1983 at the European Organisation for Nuclear Research (CERN) at Geneva in Switzerland.

4 *'Pions'* are the messenger particles for the 'strong' force, a nuclear force that holds the nucleus together. Quantum electrodynamics laid the foundations for quantum chromodynamics, which gives a quantum description of the strong force. At its heart is the proposal by M. Gellman and G. Zweig that fundamental particles called quarks make up larger particles called hadrons (including protons, neutrons, etc.). Quantum chromodynamics has met with considerable experimental success, but it still requires more confirmation before it can be fully accepted.

The Big Bang theory

In 1929 the American astronomer E.P.Hubble (1889–1953) observed that the stars are accelerating away from each other as if recoiling from a cosmic explosion. This phenomenon inspired the Big Bang theory, the hypothesis that the universe is in a state of expansion after emanating violently from a single source many billions of years ago. Confirmation of the theory came many years later in 1964 with the detection of cosmic background radiation, which was soon recognised to be residual warmth left over from the explosion. Experiments confirmed that the universe is indeed cooling down.

Attempts to gain a deeper understanding of the origin and evolution of the universe have been made by calculating the temperatures that must have existed at the time of the Big Bang and asking what the particle physics of matter must have been like at these temperatures. From his observations Hubble was able to calculate the age of the universe. The cosmic background radiation has a temperature of 3.5 degrees Kelvin and it is cooling at a measurable rate. It has been possible to extrapolate backwards and determine that the temperature of the universe less than a hundredth of a second after the bang was 10^{11} (100,000,000,000) degrees Kelvin.

A first attempt at applying particle physics to this early universe assumed that it was simply a hot soup composed mainly of electrons, positrons, neutrinos, antineutrinos and photons mingled with a smaller number of protons and neutrons. Each particle was assumed to give rise to a specific form of radiation obeying the laws of thermodynamic equilibrium. After 100,000 years the universe started to make the transition from its early radiation-dominated state to its present mass-dominated state, but there was a lapse of another 500,000 years before electrons could fall into orbit around nuclei and form atoms. From then on, under the force of gravity, galaxies and star clusters formed, and the universe gradually developed into its present state.

Later, more advanced models in particle physics were used. These do not reach their fundamental limits until pushed much closer to the zero moment of the bang. More understanding of the relationship between quantum mechanics and the gravitational force will be required before we can see into the time before 10^{-43} (0.0000000000000000000000000000000000000000001) seconds after the beginning of the universe, but grand unified field theories say that, from then up to about 10^{-35} (0.00000000000000000000000000000000001) seconds after the beginning, gravity and one other force existed, and then the strong force began to separate from the latter. At around 10^{-10} (0.0000000001) seconds, the remaining unified force is thought to have separated into the weak force and the electromagnetic force. At a millionth of a second (0.000001 seconds), a small number of hadrons (protons, neutrons, etc.) are thought to have been formed from combinations of quarks.

Before the Big Bang, a superheated melted vacuum is thought to have existed, filled with a sea of ghost particles. This vacuum cooled quickly as it expanded, and regions of it were locked into an unstable energy state such as can be observed in water when it is cooled quickly; instead of becoming ice immediately, it adopts an unstable supercooled state. A curious feature of the vacuum is its property of negative pressure, by which an effect similar to antigravity is produced – an explosive repulsive effect forcing particles apart. According to 'inflationary' models, this would explain the physical mechanism behind the Big Bang. One model sees expanding bubbles formed within the vacuum in this way, each travelling at the speed of light, each representing a different universe growing exponentially in size.

A New Physics and a New Religion

Within the extensive volumes of Bahá'í literature can be found *Some Answered Questions,* a book compiled from a series of informal talks given by 'Abdu'l-Bahá in 1906. It contains some remarkable insights suggesting that the revelations that the Bahá'í Faith makes about physical reality are in profound harmony with the most recent findings of physics. The spirit of today's scientific search for a unified field theory is anticipated in 'Abdu'l-Bahá's assertions that nature is governed by one Universal law[3] which is in operation from the invisible atom to the stars.[4] The interconnected universe implied by many theories in modern physics also seems to have been envisaged, and a chapter entitled 'The Universe Is without

Beginning' includes a description bearing a great resemblance to current theories of the Big Bang.

The universal body

Addressing a question about the 'influence of the stars', 'Abdu'l-Bahá discounts astrology, but goes on to liken the universe to a human body whose members are interconnected:

> With regard to the spiritual influence of stars, though this influence of stars in the human world may appear strange, still, if you reflect deeply upon this subject, you will not be so much surprised at it. My meaning is not, however, that the decrees which the astrologers of former times inferred from the movements of the stars corresponded to occurrences; for the decrees of those former astrologers were forms of imagination which were originated by Egyptian, Assyrian, and Chaldean priests, nay, rather, they were due to the fancies of Hindus, to the myths of the Greeks, Romans, and other star-worshippers. But I mean that this limitless universe is like the human body, all the members of which are connected and linked with one another with the greatest strength. How much the organs, the members, and the parts of the body of man are intermingled and connected for mutual aid and help, and how much they influence one another! In the same way, the parts of this infinite universe have their members and elements connected with one another, and influence one another spiritually and materially.[4]

Although the same phenomena may be implied by the 'Big Birth' (see below), here 'Abdu'l-Bahá goes further and indicates that universal interconnection or communication is present for the mutual aid and help of its member parts. He likens the complete universe to a living organism. He also states that the interconnection is not only material but also spiritual.

In another paragraph 'Abdu'l-Bahá argues that although the scientific knowledge of 1906 could not confirm universal interconnections, this did not mean that they do not exist:

> Since this connection, this spiritual effect and this influence exists between the members of the body of man, who is only one of

many finite beings, certainly between these universal and infinite beings there will also be a spiritual and material connection. Although by existing rules and actual science these connections cannot be discovered, nevertheless their existence between all beings is certain and absolute.[5]

The Big Birth

'Abdu'l-Bahá teaches that in a sense the universe is without end but also that there are universes within, such as ours, which begin and end. The description of such universes is very much like a bubble theory of the Big Bang. First he asserts the endlessness of the universe:

> it is one of the most abstruse spiritual truths that the world of existence – that is to say, this endless universe – has no beginning.[6]

The explanation given for this is that the non-existence of space and time would disprove the existence of God. Since a creator is implied by the creation, then it follows that absolute non-existence leads to the non-existence of a creator:

> an educator without pupils cannot be imagined, a monarch without subjects cannot exist, a master without scholars cannot be appointed, a creator without a creature is impossible, a provider without those provided for cannot be conceived; for all the divine names and attributes demand the existence of beings. If we could imagine a time when no beings existed, this imagination would be the denial of the Divinity of God. Moreover, absolute non-existence cannot become existence. If the beings were absolutely non-existent, existence would not have come into being. Therefore, as the Essence of Unity, that is the existence of God, is everlasting and eternal – that is to say, it has neither beginning nor end – it is certain that this world of existence, this endless universe, has neither beginning nor end.[7]

'Abdu'l-Bahá speaks of the universe being composed of globes which have a definite beginning and end; each globe is in the process of decomposition. He also speaks of an endless number of globes and states – while some globes may completely disintegrate, there are always others that exist, in keeping with his statement of the perpetuity of existence:

> Yes, it may be that one of the parts of the universe, one of the globes, for example, may come into existence, or may be disintegrated, but the other endless globes are still existing; the universe would not be disordered nor destroyed. On the contrary, existence is eternal and perpetual. As each globe has a beginning, necessarily it has an end, because every composition, collective or particular, must of necessity be decomposed. The only difference is that some are quickly decomposed, and others more slowly, but it is impossible that a composed thing should not eventually be decomposed.[8]

'Abdu'l-Bahá goes on to describe the creation of each globe, each sub-universe, and says that each emanates from a single separate source. He describes the evolution of 'one matter' which appeared in 'different aspects' giving different 'elements' which 'combined in infinite forms' to give innumerable 'beings'. This process did not happen immediately, but gradually passed through different phases until it reached its present state. Hence 'Abdu'l-Bahá equates the creation of a single globe and its development with the existence of our own universe:

> It is necessary, therefore, that we should know what each of the important existences was in the beginning – for there is no doubt that in the beginning the origin was one: the origin of all numbers is one and not two. Then it is evident that in the beginning matter was one, and that one matter appeared in different aspects of each element. Thus various forms were produced, and these various aspects as they were produced became permanent, and each element was specialised. But this permanence was not definite, and did not attain realisation and perfect existence until after a very long time. Then these elements became composed, and organised and combined in infinite forms; or rather from the composition and combination of these elements innumerable beings appeared.[9]

The description of the development of each sub-universe globe can be seen to have direct analogues in modern theories of the Big Bang in astronomy. The 'combination of infinite forms' of each element for example, could describe the infinite statistical thermodynamic inter-actions between the elementary particles of modern physics. The subsequent annihilation of particle pairs through such interactions gives rise to the eventual production of more complex particles (hadrons), which in turn gradually form familiar atoms such as hydrogen.

The Bahá'í writings, however, go much further than a material-istic description of the universe. In the same chapter 'Abdu'l-Bahá likens the development of the universe to the gradual evolution of an organism, and universal creation to the birth of an organism:

> From the composition and combination of elements, from their decomposition, from their measure, and from the effect of other beings upon them, resulted forms, endless realities, and innumerable beings. But it is clear that this terrestrial globe in its present form, did not come into existence all at once; but that this universal existence gradually passed through different phases until it became adorned with its present perfection. Universal beings resemble and can be compared to particular beings, for both are subjected to one natural system, one universal law and divine organisation. So you will find the smallest of atoms in the universal system are similar to the greatest beings of the universe. It is clear that they come into existence from one laboratory of might under one natural system and one universal law; therefore, they may be compared to one another. Thus the embryo of man in the womb of the mother gradually grows and develops, and appears in different forms and conditions, until in the degree of perfect beauty it reaches maturity and appears in a perfect form with the utmost grace. And in the same way, the seed of this flower which you see was in the beginning an insignificant thing, and very small; and it grew and developed in the womb of the earth and, after appearing in various forms, came forth in this condition with perfect freshness and grace. In the same manner it is evident that this terrestrial globe having once found its existence, grew and developed in the matrix of the universe, and came forth in different forms and conditions, until gradually it attained this present perfection, and became adorned with innumberable beings, and appeared as a finished organisation.[10]

The implication behind these assertions is that the universe is organic and it grew according to precise laws like the genetic code of a living being. Modern physics is already developing theories that point in this direction, but it has a long way to go before it can confirm such a statement.

Complementarity in Science and Religion

Science for the first time seems to describe the Universe as one system, a system that is evolving to ever higher orders of complexity. Matter and space-time are seen to be intriguing patterns of energy which constantly change form providing unseen connections throughout the cosmos. Science now has a picture of the underlying, higher order of symmetry that lies behind all forces, that characterises the seemingly infinite variety of events we see. Gradually, physics is uncovering deeper and deeper connections in the Universal System. It is also beginning to see the limits and relativity of our own sphere of existence, one that is embedded in a multitude of other dimensions and worlds.

Our world seems to be a fleeting shadow in the orb of an infinitely complex existence. What appeared to be a vacuum in fact seems to be alive with pulsating patterns of energy. It is as if scientists were uncovering the arteries and veins of a universal body, one that was destined to evolve, thus giving our own existence and place in the order of things some meaning. This rich, multi-faceted picture now being drawn by modern physics, of a universe that resembles a highly adaptable, changing and evolving organism, is very different from the cold mechanical clock of former times.

Restoring the ancient harmony
In this book we have come full circle. Ancient scientists seeking oneness, a unified coherent explanation of nature, saw no fault in combining their observations of nature with insights into the spiritual dimension that underlies the material world. To advance towards a method for investigating nature, historical circumstances made it necessary for science to fight against religious orthodoxy and also to seek inspiration in the lifeless model of the machine. This

stage in the development of science was indispensable, but it has distorted our conception of life. Even though our delvings into biology reveal to us more and more remarkable and mysteriously goal-orientated structures, many scientists feel moved – out of a feeling that only the model which made a scientific method possible can be scientific – to reduce all life phenomena to the workings of blind machinery. This loyalty to the past can now be seen to be misplaced, and the model can now be seen to be outdated. We have once again reached the point where those closest to finding a unified and coherent explanation for nature see nothing unscientific in the assumption of a divine and creative force at work within it.

As the cutting edge of science moves deeper into the nature of matter and the cosmos, physicists are not reminded of the soulless machine to which biologists would reduce the living organism. The cosmos, rather, reminds them of a living organism with a directed evolutionary development. The evolution of the universe and of our life in it has been seen to be critically dependent on fifteen or more universal constants. Even slight deviations from their numerical values would have resulted in a completely different universe or no universe at all. Many physicists have commented on how finely tuned our universe is to produce life, and they have pointed to the staggering improbability of the universe developing in the way that it has. Some have suggested that an anthropomorphic principle, a principle of intelligent creation and design, must be at work, creating universes in order to create life. This suggestion has many versions, and has received much criticism for not advancing scientific understanding, but it has been made and discussed by such eminent physicists as S. Hawkins, J. Wheeler and Fred Hoyle, as well as many others. It is frequently commented on in summaries of current theories of the Big Bang.

The indeterminacy principle of quantum mechanics and the principle of complementarity that it requires physics to employ have suggested a wider complementarity. The original scientific revolution inspired us to seek one determinate way of describing our world and ourselves. But if physics has now had to abandon this ambition, and finds greater explanatory power in the acceptance of seemingly contradictory dualities, then perhaps we may seek wisdom in a greater tolerance of such dualities elsewhere. There may be a truth to be found in reducing organisms to the mechanical parts that make them up; but there may also be a truth in the position that insists that the whole organism is greater than the sum of its parts. The greatest truth is perhaps to be found in accepting each of these approaches as an aspect of what it is to understand life. This may be the spirit in which we should approach the apparent contradictions between individual and society, between competition and co-opera-tion, between the material and the immaterial.

The rejection of the old spirit of conflict between science and religion, in favour of a new spirit of complementarity, is illustrated by Gary Zukav, author of *The Dancing Wu Li Masters*, who writes:

Acceptance without proof is the fundamental characteristic of western religion. Rejection without proof is the fundamental characteristic of western science. In other words, religion has become a matter for the heart and science has become a matter for the mind. This regrettable state of affairs does not reflect the fact that, psychologically, one cannot exist without the other. Every-body needs both. Mind and heart are only different aspects of us.[11]

Albert Einstein himself said:

Religion without science is blind. Science without religion is lame.[12]

These two approaches to wisdom are like our two eyes, left and right. Cover either one, and the picture we receive of reality is a two-dimensional distortion. Use them together in harmony, and we see the world in perspective. 'Abdu'l-Bahá, who has somehow been able to see what science can now confirm, has taught us what the third dimension is that science and religion together will show us – it is a universal and lasting peace.

NOTES

Introduction
1 'Abdu'l-Bahá, Paris Talks, London, Bahá'í Publishing Trust, 1912, p. 143.
2 See, for example, W.S. Hatcher and J.D. Martin, The Bahá'í Faith: The Emerging Global Religion, San Francisco, Harper & Row, 1984; and J. Huddleston, The Earth is but One Country, London, Bahá'í Publishing Trust, 1976.

Discovering the Material World
1 Quoted in The Galileo Affair by O. Ginerich, Scientific American, August 1982.
2 Quoted in Galileo and the Scientific Revolution by L. Fermi and G. Bernardini, New York, Basic Books Inc., 1961, p. 79.
3 Ibid., p. 80.
4 P. Davis, God and the New Physics, Harmondsworth, Pelican, 1984, p. 1–8.
5 See, for example, The World Order of Bahá'u'lláh by Shoghi Effendi, Wilmette, Bahá'í Publishing Trust, 1974, p. 20.
6 The Second Letter of Paul to the Corinthians 3:6, King James' version.
7 See Selections from the Writings of 'Abdu'l-Bahá, Haifa, Bahá'í World Centre, 1978, p. 30.
8 'Abdu'l-Bahá, Paris Talks, p. 144.
9 'Abdu'l-Bahá, Foundations of World Unity, Wilmette, Bahá'í Publishing Trust, 1971, p. 60.
10 'Abdu'l-Bahá, Paris Talks, p. 144–5.

11 'Abdu'l-Bahá, The Promulgation of Universal Peace, Wilmette, Bahá'í Publishing Trust, 1982, p. 287.

12 'Abdu'l-Bahá, Paris Talks, p. 146.

13 Ibid., p. 143.

14 Bahá'u'lláh, The Seven Valleys and the Four Valleys, Wilmette, Bahá'í Publishing Trust, 1952, p. 49.

15 Shoghi Effendi, The World Order of Bahá'u'lláh, p. xi (1938 ed.)

Human Evolution

1 See J.C. Willis, The Course of Evolution by Divergence of Mutation, Cambridge University Press, 1940.

2 See N. Elgredge and S.J. Gould, Phylogenetic Patterns and the Evolutionary Process, Columbia University Press, 1960.

3 J. Monod, Chance and Necessity, London, Collins, 1972, p. 110.

4 Ibid., p. 129–130.

5 Quoted in A New Science of Life by R. Sheldrake, London, Granada, 1983, p. 17.

6 R. Dawkins, The Selfish Gene, Oxford University Press, 1976, p. x.

7 K. Lorenz, Behind the Mirror, London, Methuen, 1977, p. 4.

8 K. Popper, Conjectures and Refutations, London, Routledge Kegan Paul, 1963.

9 Quoted in The Limits of Science by P. Medawar, Oxford University Press, 1985.

10 P. Medawar, The Limits of Science, p. 66.

11 See J. Rifkin, Algeny: A New Word – A New World, Harmondsworth, Penguin, 1984; and R. Sheldrake, A New Science of Life.

12 F. Hoyle, The Intelligent Universe, London, Dorling Kindersley, 1983, p. 25.

13 Monod, Chance and Necessity, p. 30.

14 K. Popper, Objective Knowledge: An Evolutionary Approach, Oxford University Press, 1972, p. 291–2.

15 A. Koestler and J.R. Smythies (eds.), Beyond Reductionism, London, Hutchinson, 1969, p. 1–2.

16 D. Morris, The Human Zoo, New York, Dell, 1981, p. 15.

17 Ibid., p. 53.
18 See 'Abdu'l-Bahá, Some Answered Questions, Wilmette, Bahá'í Publishing Trust, 1981.
19 'Abdu'l-Bahá, Some Answered Questions, p. 208.
20 Ibid., p. 229.
21 J.E. Esslemont, Bahá'u'lláh and the New Era, London, Bahá'í Publishing Trust, 1974, p. 147.
22 Conversation between 'Abdu'l-Bahá and Dr Fallscheer, recorded in Sonne der Warheit, No. 1, March 1921, p. 9.
23 'Abdu'l-Bahá, Some Answered Questions, p. 193.
24 See, for example, Rifkin, Algeny: A New Word.
25 'Abdu'l-Bahá, Foundations of World Unity, p. 9–10.
26 Shoghi Effendi, The World Order of Bahá'u'lláh, p. 202.
27 Ibid., p. 169.
28 See, for example, Call to the Nations by Shoghi Effendi, Haifa, Bahá'í World Centre, 1977.
29 Shoghi Effendi, The World Order of Bahá'u'lláh, p. 40.
30 See Universal House of Justice, The Promise of World Peace, London, Oneworld Publications, 1986.

The Meeting of Two Ways

 1 See F. Capra, The Tao of Physics, Hounslow, Wilwood House, 1975; and G. Zukav, The Dancing Wu Li Masters: An Overview of the New Physics, London, Rider, 1979.
 2 This is not the only explanation. Refer to N. Herbert, Quantum Reality; Beyond the New Physics, London, Rider, 1985.
 3 'Abdu'l-Bahá, Some Answered Questions, p. 3.
 4 Ibid., p. 245.
 5 Ibid., p. 246–7.
 6 Ibid., p. 180.
 7 Ibid.
 8 Ibid., p. 180–1.
 9 Ibid.
10 Ibid., p. 182.
11 Zukav, The Dancing Wu Li Masters, p. 110.
12 A. Einstein, Ideas and Opinions, London, Souvenir Press, 1973, p. 46.

BIBLIOGRAPHY

'Abdu'l-Bahá, Paris Talks, Addresses given by 'Abdu'l-Bahá in Paris in 1911–12. London, Bahá'í Publishing Trust, 1912. 11th ed. 1969.

———, The Promulgation of Universal Peace, Talks delivered by 'Abdu'l-Bahá during his visit to the United States and Canada in 1912. Wilmette, Bahá'í Publishing Trust, 2nd ed. 1982.

———, Selections from the Writings of 'Abdu'l-Bahá, Haifa, Bahá'í World Centre, 1978.

———, Some Answered Questions, Wilmette, Bahá'í Publishing Trust, 3rd ed. 1981.

———, Foundations of World Unity, Compiled from Addresses and Tablets of 'Abdu'l-Bahá, Wilmette, Bahá'í Publishing Trust, 1945.

Adler, R., Bazin, M. and Shiffer, M. Introduction to General Relativity, McGraw-Hill, 1965.

Aspect, A., Dalibard, J. and Roger, G. Experimental Test of Bell's Inequalities Using Time-Varying Analyzers, Physical Review Letters, Vol 49, No. 25, Dec. 1982.

Bohm, D. Wholeness and the Implicate Order, London, Routledge and Kegan Paul, 1980.

Boslough, J. Beyond the Black Hole, London, Collins, 1985.

Cagnac, B. and Pebay-Peyroula, J. Modern Atomic Physics, The Macmillan Press, 1975.

Capra, F. Tao of Physics, Hounslow, Wilwood House, 1975.

———, The Turning Point, Hounslow, Wilwood House, 1982.

Close, F. The Cosmic Onion, London, Heinemann Educational, 1983.

Cohen, B. The Birth of a New Physics, London, Heinemann, 1960.

Coley, N. and Hal, V. (eds.), Primary Sources on Science and Belief, London, Longman, 1980.

Davies, P. God and New Physics, London, Dent, 1983.

——, Other Worlds, London, Dent, 1980.

——, Superforce, London, Unwin, 1985.

——, The Accidental Universe, Cambridge University Press, 1982.

Dawkins, R. The Selfish Gene, Oxford University Press, 1976.

Eisberg, R. Fundamentals of Modern Physics, Chichester, John Wiley.

Esslemont, J.E. Bahá'u'lláh and the New Era, London, Bahá'í Publishing Trust, 1974.

Gingerich, O. The Galileo Affair, Scientific American, August, 1982.

Gould, S. Ever Since Darwin, Pelican, 1980.

Gribbin, J. In Search of the Double Helix, London, Corgi, 1985.

——, In Search of Schrödinger's Cat, Hounslow, Wilwood House, 1984.

Hatcher, W.S. The Science of Religion, Ontario, The Canadian Association for Studies on the Bahá'í Faith, 1977.

Hayes, J.R. (ed.) The Genius of Arab Civilisation, London, Phaidon, 1978.

Heisenberg, W. Physics and Beyond, London, Harper & Row, 1971.

Hoyle, F. The Intelligent Universe, USA, Dorling Kindersley, 1983.

Jones, R. Physics as Metaphor, Hounslow, Wilwood House, 1983.

Koestler, A. and Smythies, J. (eds.) Beyond Reductionism, London, Hutchinson, 1969.

Lorenz, K. Behind the Mirror, London, Methuen, 1977.

——, On Aggression, London, Methuen, 1979.

Marks, J. Science and the Making of Modern World, London, Heinemann Educational, 1983.

Medawar, P. The Limits of Science, Oxford University Press, 1985.

Monod, J. Chance and Necessity, London, Collins, 1972.

Morris, D. The Human Zoo, USA, Dell, 1981.

Motlagh, H. (Comp.) Unto Him Shall We Return, Wilmette, Bahá'í Publishing Trust, 1985.

Polkinghome, J. The Quantum World, London, Longman, 1984.

Popper, K.R. Objective Knowledge, Oxford University Press, 1972.

Quigg, C. Elementary Particles and Forces, Scientific American, April 1985.

Rafelski, J. and Muller, B. The Structured Vacuum, Verlag Harri Deutch, 1985.

Rhodes, F. The Evolution of Life, Harmondsworth, Penguin, 1976.

Rifkin, J. Algeny: A New Word — A New World, Harmondsworth, Penguin, 1984.

Russell, B. A History of Western Philosophy, London, Unwin, 1946.

Schiff, L. Quantum Mechanics, McGraw-Hill, 1955.

Sheldrake, R. A New Science of Life, London, Granada, 1983.

Shoghi Effendi, The World Order of Bahá'u'lláh, Wilmette, Bahá'í Publishing Trust, 1974.

Stanley, S.M. The New Evolutionary Timetable, New York, Basic Books, 1981.

Universal House of Justice, The Promise of World Peace, London, Oneworld Publications, 1986.

Weinberg, S. The First Three Minutes, London, André Deutch, 1977.

Zukav, G. The Dancing Wu Li Masters, London, Rider, 1979.

INDEX

'Abdu'l-Bahá 4, 50, 51, 88, 89, 90

Abraham 49

absolute proof 67

aggression 82, 83, 84, 98

alchemists 40

Alhazen 23

Anaximander 7–8

Anaximenes 7–8

animals, human beings as 64, 73–4, 80, 83, 84, 86, 89

anticlericalism 58

antimatter 108–9

Archimedes 15, 28

Aristarchus 14, 29

Aristotle 13–15, 16, 23, 24, 25, 26, 28, 29, 32, 33, 35, 36, 38, 40, 57

Arius 18, 19

arms race 84

Aspect, Alan 108

astrology 113

astronomy 14, 23, 29, 36, 40, 56

atomic theory 13, 40, 106

atoms 12, 30, 33, 43, 103–4

Avicenna 24, 90

Bahá'í Faith 3, 4, 49–54, 87–98, 99, 112–9

Bahá'u'lláh 52, 97, 99

belief 52, 67, 69, 72

Bell inequality 108

Bible 25, 31, 32, 41, 47–8, 56, 57, 58, 59, 65, 66, 80, 85, 90

Big Bang 111–2, 113, 114, 115, 118

biology 56, 64–5, 66, 70, 77, 78, 99

Bohm, David 106–7

Bohr, Niels 106

botany 61

Brahe, Tycho 29, 30, 37, 44

Bruno, Giordano 30

Buddha 49

Buddhism 99

Byzantine Empire 19, 21, 22

capitalism 82, 95

Carnegie, Andrew 82

Casimir effect 109

Catholicism 30, 32, 35, 36, 85

chance 3, 56, 64, 65, 71, 75, 85, 87, 90

chance-and-necessity 72, 74, 76

chemistry 40

Christ 26, 49, 52

Christianity 7, 17–21, 24, 26, 40, 44, 46–8, 51, 53, 58, 85

chromosomes 62, 63, 79

Church 2, 5, 15, 18–21, 24–7, 28, 30, 31, 36, 40, 41, 46–8, 58, 85

civilisation 82, 88, 92, 95

Clauser, J. 108

competition 82

complementarity 100, 117–8

computer program analogy 62, 79

Comte, Auguste 58

consciousness 76

Constantine 19, 20

Constantinople 19, 24

Copenhagen interpretation 106

Copernicus, Nicolas 29, 30, 31, 35, 36, 37

Counter-Reformation 15, 27

creation 25, 31, 36, 46, 48, 56, 57, 65, 78, 90, 114

cultural progress 92

Dalton, John 40

Darwin, Charles 59–62, 65, 72, 80, 82, 90

data 13, 27, 42, 43, 67, 69

da Vinci, Leonardo 28

Dawkins, Richard 65

de Broglie, Louis 105

Democritus 12, 43

Descartes, René 33, 35–6, 37, 38, 54, 76

design 71, 72, 73, 76, 78, 87, 90, 91, 92, 100, 118

determinism 54, 56, 80–3

dialectical materialism 81

dialectics 80

Dionysian cults 7

Dirac equation 106, 108

DNA 62, 63, 71, 73

doctrine of Christian Church 19, 21, 27, 40, 44, 57, 85

dogma 37, 44, 45, 46, 50, 51, 80, 85

dynamics 13, 34

Egypt 16

Einstein, Albert 40, 101, 102, 104, 106, 108, 109, 110, 119

electricity 40, 41, 70

electromagnetism 70, 110

elements 8, 9, 43

engineering 28, 32, 41

EPR experiment 106–7, 112

evolution 3, 55–98

Faraday 40, 41

forces 38, 110

Forms 11, 13, 15, 28, 40

fossils 57, 62, 63, 66, 75

Freedman, S. 108

freedom 95

Galileo 26, 27, 30–5, 36, 37, 57, 85, 99

Galton, Francis 61

Gellman, M. 110

genes 61, 62, 63, 65
genetics 62
geology 57, 59, 66
ghost particles 112
global community 55, 83, 97
goal-directedness 78
God, existence of 36, 52, 67,
  68, 69, 114
gradualism 62, 63, 75
gravity 37, 38, 103, 110
Greek thought 2, 5, 6–15, 20,
  21, 22, 24, 25, 26, 28, 30,
  43, 47, 56, 57, 85

Hawkins, S. 118
Hegel, G. W. F. 9, 80
Heisenberg, W. K. 105, 107,
  109
Heraclides 14
Heraclitus 9
Herz 41
history 83
Hoyle, Fred 71–2, 118
Hubble, E. P. 111
human behaviour 74
humanism 25
human mind 69
human nature 65, 86
human society 92
human species, development of
  91
human spirit 87–9, 98
Hutton, James 57–8, 59
Huxley, Julian 62
Huxley, Thomas 65
hypothesis 42, 43, 66, 67, 68,
  69, 70, 71, 72

idealism 83
Industrial Revolution 41
Inquisition 26, 30, 31, 36
instinct 82
interconnections 112, 113
Islam 3, 5, 7, 19, 21–4, 27, 40,
  41, 48, 53

Jews 17, 18, 19, 24, 41
jungle model 81–3, 86

Kepler, Johannes 36, 37, 44
Koestler, Arthur 77
Kosmos 8, 9, 12

Lamarck, Jean Baptiste 58, 61
light 103, 104–5
Lightfoot, Dr 57
Locke 33
Lorentz, H. A. 102
Lorenz, Konrad 65
Lyell, Charles 59

machines, humans as 36, 65, 76
magnetism 40, 41, 70
Malthus, Thomas 59
Marconi 41
Marx, Karl 9, 80–2
materialism 4, 12, 36, 56, 57,
  65, 69, 78
materialistic determinism 54
mathematics 5, 10, 23, 24, 28,
  33, 36
matter 11, 14, 26, 32, 33, 40
Maxwell, James Clerk 40, 70,
  103, 110
mechanics 15, 32, 37
mechanistic determinism 3

Medawar, Peter 68
medicine 24, 41
Mendel, Gregor 61
messenger particles 110
Michelson-Morley experiment
   101
Middle Ages 5, 24, 27, 47
molecular biology 62
Monod, Jacques 64, 66, 72, 78
morality 84–6
Morris, Desmond 82
Moses 49, 90
motion, laws of 37–8
Muḥammad 22, 23, 49
mutation 62, 63, 78

natural selection 60, 62, 72, 75
Newton, Sir Isaac 31, 32, 34,
   36–9, 54, 57, 101, 102, 110
New World Order 95
nihilism 80

objectivity 66–7, 68, 71, 72,
   73, 83, 84, 85, 99
observation 15, 27, 31, 33, 42,
   43, 57
organic world civilisation 95
origin of life 68
Orphic religion 7, 10, 12

palaeontology 61–2
Parmenides 9, 13
particle theory 105
peace 83, 84, 94, 95, 96, 97
physics 25, 28, 32, 33, 35, 40,
   64, 70, 77, 78, 99, 101, 110
Planck, Max 104

planetary system 14, 20, 23,
   26, 29–30, 35, 36, 37, 38,
   44, 56
Plato 9, 10, 11, 12, 13, 14, 15,
   20, 21, 25, 26, 28, 29, 33
Plotinus 20
Podolsky, B. 106
popes 19, 20, 21, 25, 26, 31
Popper, Karl 66, 68, 77
positivism, 58, 68
Priestly, Joseph 37
priests 18, 21, 26, 39, 42, 85
Protestantism 26, 30, 35
punctuationists 61, 63, 75
purpose 48, 67, 68, 71, 72, 73,
   75, 78, 79, 87, 88, 98
Pythagoras 10, 90

quantum theory 104, 105, 106,
   107, 112, 118

rational soul 88
realism 83, 84, 86
reality 11, 12, 27, 36, 108
reason 9, 32, 37, 50, 52
reductions 8, 43, 48, 70–8, 85,
   86, 100
Reformation 26
relativity 40, 102, 106, 110
religious inquiry 44–6
Renaissance 15, 23, 24, 25, 26,
   28, 29, 32, 42
Romans 16, 17, 18, 19, 20, 22,
   25, 26
Rosen, N. 106

Saint-Simon, Comte de 58
Salam, A. 110

Schrödinger, Erwin 105, 106
science, limits of 49, 67–9
scientific method 2, 5, 12, 13,
    27, 32, 41, 42–4, 48, 50,
    52, 53–4, 56, 66, 67, 70, 72
scientific revolutions 5, 12, 13,
    15, 40, 41, 42, 54, 55, 99,
    100
Shoghi Effendi 52, 94
social determinism 80–3
socialism 95
social principles 53
social sciences 80
Socrates 10, 11
solar system, *see* planetary
    system
soul 36, 76, 87, 88
space 101, 102
Sparnay, M. J. 109
Spencer, Herbert 58, 82
spirit, *see* human spirit
spiritual 48, 53, 92
statics 13, 15
St Augustine 20, 21, 29
stochastic electrodynamics 109
St Thomas Aquinas 25, 57
supernatural 8, 12
superstition 4, 51, 72, 80
survival 3, 64, 65, 82, 83, 84,
    85, 86, 87, 95, 96
survival of the fittest 56, 60, 89
synthesis, modern 62, 64, 70,
    77, 78, 79

Taoism 99
teleological paradox 79
teleological principle 80, 91, 92
telescope 29, 30
Thales 7
theocracy 18, 19, 26, 30
time 101, 102
transcendental purpose 75
truth 46, 49, 52

uncertainty principle 105, 107,
    109
unified field theory 70, 109,
    112
Unitarianism 37
universe 3, 38, 48, 54, 111,
    112, 117, 118
Ussher, Archbishop James 57

Wallace, Alfred Russel 60
wave theory 105
Weinberg, S. 110
Wheeler, J. 118
world government 98
world unity 86, 94

Zeno of Elea 9
zoology 58
Zukov, Gary 119
Zweig, G. 110